CASH IS KING

Investing in REIT Preferreds
To Generate Long-term Income

BY

SIMON
WADSWORTH

Published in the United States by BookMasters, Inc.

ISBN: 978-0-692-01396-0
Library of Congress Control Number: 2011906253

www.simonwadsworth.com

Acknowledgements

A lot of people have helped me with this book. The most important are the three people who provided me with the opportunity and knowledge to write it: George Cates, who founded Mid-America Apartments, made it very successful, and gave me the opportunity to be CFO, and Eric Bolton, his successor as CEO, who took the Company to the next level of success. My wife, Jill, has been very supportive of it as part of my transition from the busy day-to-day life of a CFO to the more varied existence of work and travel.

Ed Wiley of SS+D Financial provided much of the analysis and insights on hedging and on the relative performance of my REIT Preferred portfolio. He also helped me with many ideas and suggestions on the content and structure. The impressive REIT Research team at Raymond James were also a huge help, especially Alex Sierra with his quarterly REIT Preferred analysis, and Brad Butcher of the investment banking team at Raymond James who kept me abreast of the latest developments. The Bank of Montreal research team continued to support me with their weekly statistical updates. Three excellent books on Preferred stock and Preferred stock investing by Kenneth Winans, Paul Josephs, and Doug Le Du were also very helpful.

Susan Drake of Spellbinders helped me enormously with advice, editing, and the production of the book, and took a raw product and made it into something.

Other friends who gave up a lot of time to help were Don Hutson of US Learning Systems, Greer Simonton, and Phil Ashford who provided me with ideas, suggestions, and other important support.

Finally, the views expressed in this book are those of the author alone.

"Simon Wadsworth's knowledge of how to make money in REITs is unparalleled. If you miss this read, you may well miss your best profit opportunity of the year! Congratulations on a terrific book, Simon."

Don Hutson
Co-Author of NY Times International Best-Sellers
The One Minute Entrepreneur &
The One Minute Negotiator
Author, Sales Growth Specialist, CEO
U.S. Learning, Inc.

CASH IS KING
Investing in REIT Preferreds
To Generate Long-term Income

Table Of Contents

CHAPTER 1
Where's My Nest Egg?

The Stock Market Pessimist sees the glass as half empty.
The Optimist sees the glass half full. The short-term Trader
JUST ADDS WHISKEY...

Many of my friends who are in the "bulge bracket" age group (55-65) are concerned about having adequate income for retirement. A lucky few are covered by defined benefit pension plans, but most (and an increasing number) have only their IRAs and 401-K program, and these folks are worried. Their nest egg just isn't big enough.

Many drank the widely-disseminated Kool-Aid that long-term total returns of low double digits were reasonable expectations for the stock market. That concept was damaged after the tech bubble burst in 2001, and then was killed-off by the 2008 stock market rout. Actual equity returns over the last 10 years are now well known to have been minimal, in the 0% - 2% range on average.

Many who are already retired are facing the reality that money market and CD yields of below 1% are now the norm, and that these rates may well continue for some period of time. Some withdrew their money from the equity markets during the period of high economic uncertainty in late 2008-2010, have missed the stock market rally of late 2010, and cannot find an investment vehicle delivering cash returns which are substantially above what they believe is the rate of inflation. Some who are reducing their exposure to the stock market have embarked on risky investment strategies, locking up money in longer term Treasuries or high yield bonds with little understanding of the potential risks to the principal. As we'll review in a later chapter, in times of rising interest rates and higher inflation expectations, long-term bond prices drop, jeopardizing the principal value of the bonds. Given the large government deficits and the very loose monetary policy, there is at least a risk that inflation will rise and the dollar weaken.

During the last 10-year period it was possible to earn investment returns in the low double digits in Real Estate Investment Trust (REIT) equities, with a substantial portion in cash dividends. REIT Preferreds generated returns in the high single digits, effectively all of it in cash dividends. That's why this book is especially germane to investors looking for a nest egg.

As we survey the US investment markets, we realize that we may well be headed into an extended period of sub-par economic growth, as other parts of the world catch up and perhaps assume world economic leadership. It seems quite possible that the country will lack the political will to address its economic issues. The risks of low economic growth are at least as big as the risks of inflation. Many investment advisers now suggest that long-term stock market returns of 4% – 7% annually seem to be more realistic. In the time horizon of the retirement of the bulge bracket age group (2012 – 2017) quite possibly returns will be much less.

We also have to reckon with the increasing role of the Government and the Fed in the financial world, which has resulted in excessive volatility of shares and asset prices. It is a small wonder that there are large amounts of dollars sitting in money market funds and banks earning less than 1%, sitting on the sidelines waiting for a market pull-back, and that many investors (and especially those nearing retirement) are reluctant to hop back on the stock market roller coaster.

The growing pressure for portfolio diversification has increased the interest in alternative investments to equities. The paradigm shift of the past few years has been that many institutional investors have already diversified into hedge funds, private equity, and other non-stock market investments where they think returns will be better and more reliable, but they've had mixed results.

While younger people are working on building their net worth and are primarily interested in the upside potential of capital appreciation, people approaching retirement are concerned about protecting their investment principal and generating income. The alternative of funding an annuity to provide a steady income through retirement is looking quite unattractive: yields are very low, and will stay this way for a period of time. The other reality is that the annuity income stream is only as good as the credit of the provider, so annuities are not completely risk-free.

So, what can investors do to fill the income gap? One solution is to seek higher cash yields on their capital. Yet this has become harder and harder. World governments have used aggressive monetary policy to try to turn around stalled economic growth, so both short and long-term yields have been driven to record low levels. Annuities, municipal bonds, CDs, and Treasuries which are traditional investments for income-oriented investors all have minimal before-tax yields, made even lower after tax. After considering the long-term inflation rate, investors in these asset classes are frequently experiencing a negative yield.

So what happens if you allocate part of an investment portfolio to the preferred shares of Real Estate Investment Trusts (REIT Preferreds) can represent 5% – 15% of an investment portfolio, and provide a significant cash flow boost to an investor's current income while at the same time increasing portfolio diversification. REIT Preferreds are an investment niche that for various reasons have been overlooked and under-priced by investors, and thus have proven to be an attractive alternative to high yield bonds and to annuities.

Any investor who is reasonably involved with the management of his or her investment portfolio can follow this suggested program. This book is not intended for the passive investor or for the sophisticated institutional investor (especially those who are dedicated to income securities), but is intended for the more active investor or the investment advisor who wishes to generate a steady cash income from a more diversified investment portfolio.

CHAPTER 2

A Little Undiscovered Treasure

"Doc, I feel shortness of breath, dizziness, cold sweats, can't sleep. Do you think I will collapse any time soon?"
Doctor: "Yep. You must be from Wall Street!"

In a hidden corner of the investment market remains a relatively undiscovered investment opportunity that fits the needs of retirees needing current cash income and of investors needing fixed income diversification. Preferred shares issued by Real Estate Investment Trusts have been around since the mid-1990s, and REITs in their modern form have been around since 1993. Both the preferred and common shares of REITs have delivered excellent investment returns to investors making sound common-sense decisions.

Dividend yields for some of these REIT Preferreds are higher than they should be because of market inefficiencies. We'll explore why this occurs and develop a REIT Preferred investment strategy that balances "risk" and "return."

Preferred stocks are debt-like: They pay a fixed amount (a dividend, not interest) to the investor on a regular basis. Changes in their prices are not tied to growth in earnings but to changes in interest rates and the credit of the issuing company. In general, Preferreds are higher risk than debt, but lower risk than common equity, as they are more senior on the balance sheet. Preferred owners are more likely than owners of common shares to recover some value in the event of bankruptcy.

The purpose of this book is to lay out the basic parameters to follow to make solid cash returns by investing in REIT Preferreds. The book aims to provide you with a road map to limit risk and make investing in REIT Preferreds a successful income-generating part of any investment portfolio. Some parts of the strategy are not intuitive, but if you have modest investing experience you should be able to execute it with ease.

In this book you will learn:

- Why REIT Preferreds have been overlooked
- How you can generate a cash return in the high single digits
- Why the right portfolio of REIT Preferreds is secure
- How to identify and select the REIT Preferreds with the most upside opportunity
- How to minimize investment risks

My experience

Until my retirement from active management at the end of 2009, for 16 years I was the Chief Financial Officer and a Director of a successful publicly-traded Real Estate Investment Trust which delivered one of the top investment returns in its sector. This gave me direct experience of dealing with institutional investors, REIT capital structures, rating agencies, and REIT Preferreds.

Beginning in January 2009, I made a series of personal investments in REIT Preferreds, mostly in the latter half of 2009 and in 2010. Calculated on an internal rate of return basis, the investments returned 78% in 2009 and 33% in 2010, for an overall annualized (IRR) of 50%. Color me happy! This result was far in excess of the averages for REIT Preferreds over the same time period. Unfortunately, such spectacular investment returns cannot be repeated, but it is reasonable to expect that you can achieve more modest returns in the high single digits. My experience makes me confident of this.

8% cash yield is realistic

Following the proposed strategy, at the present time through investing in REIT Preferreds you can:

- Maintain a well-diversified portfolio that minimizes investment risk

- Generate over 8% cash return (from dividends)
- Earn a substantially better risk-adjusted return than the average for REIT Preferreds.

Given risk parameters that seem quite acceptable and the Fed's goals of containing inflation at less than 3%, an 8% yield should be highly attractive to most investors seeking income over a long period.

Many investors are looking for investment products that can generate a reasonable income, represent a reasonable diversification from pure equities and bonds, and do this without excessive risk. Many realize that annuities, with high costs and limited protection, are not necessarily the answer. At present REIT Preferreds can fill this need.

Apart from addressing the investment needs of retirees needing current income, REIT Preferreds can also fit very well as a cash income generator and a diversification alternative in a tax deferred account such as an IRA.

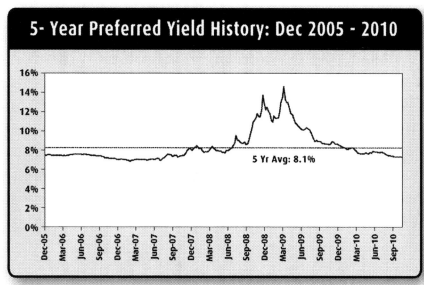

5- Year Preferred Yield History: Dec 2005 - 2010

5 Yr Avg: 8.1%

Source: Bloomberg, SNL Financial, BMO Capital Markets

Chart 1

The REIT Preferred investment sector is too small for the big players to take a serious interest

The total market for REIT Preferreds is less than $20 billion, just 6% of the $350 billion for REIT common stocks. Owners of REIT Preferreds tend to hold onto their shares, with the result that the stocks trade in low volumes, making it hard for institutional investors to move in and out of their investment positions. Retail owners, needing to trade small volumes, are not affected to the same extent. As a result, the number of institutions owning REIT Preferreds is limited. There is only one mutual fund – and no Exchange Traded Fund (ETF) – and there are no investment bank research analysts dedicated to solely REIT Preferreds.

Investors and the Rating Agencies over-weight the credit risks

As a class, REITs have been outstanding investments in their modern format; a large majority has been secure. Of the 110+ public REITs, only one filed for bankruptcy in the three-year period 2007 – 2010, which was the most difficult time for business and financing that I experienced in my 40-year business career. During that same period only three public REITs that I'm aware of suspended their preferred dividend payments, and one of these was subsequently reinstated.

For several reasons that I explain later, the greatest opportunity to buy REIT Preferreds at the best risk-adjusted price is in stocks that are:

- Not rated by the major Rating Agencies (Moody's and Standard & Poor's), or
- Rated 'below investment grade'

Rating Agencies and many investors don't get it right when it comes to rating and evaluating REIT preferred securities, and the evidence for this has been the stocks' consistent dividend paying performance.

We'll discuss why REIT Preferreds are pretty secure as an investment category: they are backed by hard assets, and issued by relatively unleveraged companies. In the event of bankruptcy (which as we have seen is extremely rare among public REITs), the chance of recovery should be greater than with other asset classes. And a broad cross-section (just over half) of all REITs has issued preferred stock.

Buy preferred shares of REITs with improving credit

Buying the preferred shares of REITs, which can be reasonably expected to improve their balance sheets, such as by reducing leverage or improve cash flow, is a simple strategy that works at two levels. It improves the opportunity for the share price to move up, and it decreases the risk of price pressure resulting from increasing interest rates. We'll review tools to help you identify these opportunities.

There are risks, but they are manageable

There are several sensible precautions to take in managing risk in any investment strategy. There are risks that are peculiar to REIT Preferreds that we'll discuss in depth, and we'll show strategies to mitigate these and to manage the portfolio appropriately.

The major risks to protect against are risky bond rates (which affect preferred pricing) and the credit risk associated with individual stocks.

The Fed has indicated that they are going to be vigilant in heading off inflation. In the face of a long period of very loose monetary policies this may be difficult to achieve. The best defenses for an income-oriented investor seeking more than the extremely low yields offered by banks and Treasuries are:

- **Diversification of investment categories:** Making an allocation to REIT Preferreds of 5% - 15% of an investment portfolio makes a lot of sense for most investors. REIT Preferreds are not going to be winners all of the time, but over the long haul they will do fine.
- **Dollar cost average:** Take a year or so to make your investments, and if you don't immediately need to use the dividend income, reinvest this.

Managing credit risk of individual companies can best be achieved through:

- **Diversification among individual REIT Preferreds:** Maintain an active portfolio of 10 – 20 stocks.

- **Looking closely at REIT Preferreds issued since October 2010:** Some of these contain worthwhile protections against principal loss resulting from takeovers.

- **Active Management:** Don't go to sleep on the portfolio; keep up with the individual companies in your portfolio and with prospective stocks. Investments in REIT Preferreds generate great dividend income, but should not be traditional 'widows and orphans' investments unless actively managed within the guidelines suggested here.

It doesn't take a lot of money

Unlike investing in common shares, the small size and relatively limited liquidity of the REIT Preferred market actually provides a comparative advantage to the smaller investor compared to the big institutions. It is hard to move a lot of money quickly. Investors with as little as $10,000 to $20,000 can build a portfolio of diverse REIT Preferreds; there is no optimum size, but portfolios of $100,000 - $5 million can be efficiently and safely managed with adequate liquidity.

REITs: A strong history of performance

Real Estate Investment Trusts were established to facilitate the ownership of real estate by the public, and have some fairly arcane structures and requirements that enable them to maintain a tax-advantaged form (simply, they don't pay corporate income tax).

Investors in their common stock have been fortunate to have experienced exceptional investment returns, much of it in cash, well in excess of equity market average. (See Chart 2) An investment of $1 at the beginning of 2000 in the Dow Jones Industrial average portfolio would be worth $1.01 at the end of 2010. The same $1 investment in REITs (the Morgan Stanley REIT Index) would be worth $2.50. The total market value of the common stock of the 110+ public REITs now approaches $350 billion, and REITs form a well-accepted category of investments.

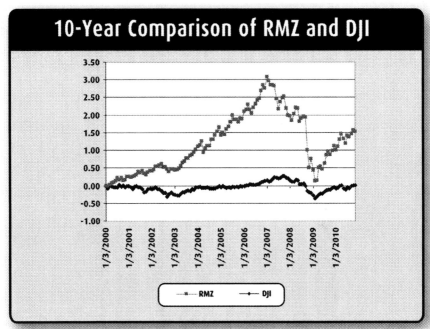

10-Year Comparison of RMZ and DJI

Legend: RMZ, DJI

Source: Bloomberg, SNL Financial, BMO Capital Markets

Chart 2

CASH IS KING

CHAPTER 3
Why REIT Preferred Shares?

Sometimes it takes several years to recognize the obvious.

REIT Preferred shares have not been appropriately recognized by the investment community, even though they represent a great investment opportunity for much of the investment cycle.

Because the REIT Preferred market is small (sub-$20 billion), most institutional analysts and investors have ignored them. Rating Agencies tend to under-rate REIT Preferred stocks, presenting a particular opportunity in this category of non-investment grade shares. And for many years sub-investment grade REIT Preferreds were regarded as poor investments which were avoided by knowledgeable institutional investors: in other words, only unscrupulous investment banks sold such securities to naïve retail investors. Reputable REITs began to issue preferred stock in the mid-1990s, generally marketed by sound investment banks with ethical track records. While certainly exhibiting some price volatility, which we'll discuss later, over the long haul a sound investment program should deliver cash returns of high single-digits with acceptable degrees of risk. The investment returns for REIT Preferred have so far been exceptional, and because of the small market size and the lack of investor recognition, returns can be expected to be superior on a risk-adjusted basis to other large-market high yield alternatives such as bonds; for this reason they should be considered as an alternative to high yield bonds in portfolio allocations.

An investor who is willing to actively manage a portfolio and accept some volatility of principal values can earn returns equal to or above what the typical stock market investor may reasonably expect, and do so primarily through generating cash dividend income (as opposed to mainly capital appreciation). Cash dividends offer the opportunity to rebalance a portfolio on a routine basis and dollar cost average or provide current income on which an investor relying on unearned income can live.

After reading this book, for reasons of time, experience, or confidence, some investors may choose to invest in REIT Preferreds through an Exchange Traded Fund or mutual fund. However, as I mentioned before, these alternatives are very limited as there are no ETFs dedicated to REIT Preferreds, and only one mutual fund. A discussion of the mutual fund alternative is included in the section on investment strategy.

CHAPTER 4

The Structure of a Modern REIT

I made a tremendous amount of money on real estate.
I'll take real estate rather than go to Wall Street
and get 2.8 percent. Forget about it.
   – Ivana Trump

Real Estate Investment Trusts have been around since Congress created the REIT structure in 1960, but have existed in their modern form since 1993. The objective of Congress was to provide public investors with the opportunity to invest in real estate with the same tax advantages held by private investors. Private real estate investors that wish to invest in high quality commercial real estate are generally required to make large direct investments, which limits this to wealthy individuals or institutions such as pension funds. Relatively few real estate partnerships are big enough to be registered with the SEC, so their ownership is required to be limited to high-net worth or high-income individuals that are exempt from buying SEC-registered securities. Public REITs, all of which are registered with the SEC, are structured to level the playing field between large rich investors and those of more moderate means.

The particular advantage provided by Congress is that a REIT operates with a similar tax structure to a private partnership: like a partnership, a REIT doesn't pay tax at the corporate level, but only on distributions paid to individual investors. Dividends are thus effectively only taxed once (as opposed to twice for regular corporations). In order to qualify for this tax-advantaged status, REITs must operate within certain constraints that we'll explore a little more in Chapter 8, which describes how taxes affect you, the preferred stock investor. One of these constraints is that REITs must distribute at least 90% of their net income in dividends, and REITs are well known for being an attractive investment vehicle for investors seeking dividend income.

A further important advantage is that private owners of commercial real estate can swap their properties for an interest in the public REIT in a tax-deferred transaction. Many REITs are structured as so-called 'UPREITs' – or Umbrella Partnership REITs.

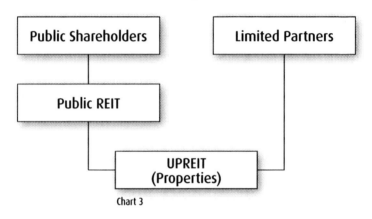

Chart 3

In these cases, the assets of the company are primarily owned by the UPREIT, a limited partnership, which is owned by a public company and by 'UPREIT holders.' These are the limited partners who have exchanged their ownership of an individual property for 'UPREIT units.' This structure generally has no important investment implications for the preferred shareholders, with the exception discussed below. It does have limited implications for public shareholders.

From an investor's perspective, REIT dividends on both their common shares and their preferred shares are taxed at shareholders' marginal tax rates, as they do not meet qualified dividend requirements that currently apply to dividend payments made by non-REIT stocks. At the time of writing, it seems likely that the tax rate on dividend payments by non-REITs may rise in the future, making REIT dividends relatively more attractive.

In addition there are 20 mortgage REITs, which specialize in financing real estate, and which are distinctly different animals. I do not plan to cover these in this book. The equity capitalization of their preferred stock is less than $1 billion, compared to $18.5 billion of Preferreds of all the other equity REITs. Mortgage REITs are finance companies as opposed to real estate owners and operators, and have a different financial structure to property-owning equity REITs.

	Corporation Type	
	Regular "C"	REIT
Net Income	100	100
Corporate Tax	-40	0
Net Income	60	100
Dividend	60	90
Investor Tax Rate	15%	36%*
Investor Tax	-9	-32.4
Cash to Investor	51	57.6

*Assumed Investor Marginal Rate
A 'Regular C' corporation is a non-REIT, tax-paying company

Chart 4

In the section on tax in Chapter 8, we'll look at the tax aspects of REIT dividends that can be highly beneficial, which can help offset partially the fact that REIT dividends do not meet qualified dividends requirements. As much as 50%, or sometimes more, of common dividends can be classified as 'return of capital' for tax purposes, often resulting in common dividends effectively being taxed at well below the investor's individual tax rate.

Existing REIT opportunities

In addition to the initial REITs which have been successfully operating since the mid-1990s, several new REITs are expected to have their initial public offerings in 2011. Just over half of these non-mortgage equity REITs have outstanding preferred stock, and these REITs are my focus.

In addition there are 20 mortgage REITs, which specialize in financing real estate, and which are distinctly different animals. I do not plan to cover these in this book. The equity capitalization of their preferred stock is less than $1 billion, compared to $18.5 billion of Preferreds of all the other equity REITs. Mortgage REITs are finance companies as opposed to real estate owners and operators, and have a different financial structure to property-owning equity REITs.

Publicly Traded Equity REITs		
Equity REITs *	$millions Total Equity Capitalization	Total Companies
Healthcare	40,200	12
Office	60,800	16
Industrial	16,200	6
Office-Industrial	16,700	8
Shopping Center	27,200	13
Malls	67,800	8
Student Housing	2,600	2
Manufactured Housing	2,800	3
Multifamily	51,200	14
Self-Storage	20,100	4
Lodging	21,400	11
Specialty/Triple Net	23,000	14
Total	350,000	111
*Excludes Mortgage REITs Source: KeyBanc 11-26-2010		
Mortgage	24,233	20

Chart 5

The publicly-owned equity REITs are generally fully integrated operating businesses that own, develop, build, buy, and sell commercial real estate. They tend to specialize in an asset class, such as offices, industrial, apartments, hotels, etc. Some REITs are quite narrow in their focus, such as facilities for medical research or nursing homes, while a few can be more geographic in their concentration, or can invest in multiple asset types.

REITs have become a well-accepted investment category with a total capitalization approaching $650 billion, of which over half is equity. The vast majority of public REITs are internally advised and managed, which has helped to reduce conflicts of interest and eliminated the need for advisory and management fees paid to third-party management groups. In the past 10 years the NAREIT equity index (a performance index of REIT shares) has a compound annual return in excess of 10%, compared to a slight negative return for the S&P 500. REIT common shares are recognized as being excellent investments for investors seeking to fund retirement, either for individuals or for defined benefit programs where income plus inflation protection is the goal. Like companies in other corporate forms, some REITs have consolidated and gone private, and the average size has increased substantially over time as the cost of being a public company has risen. Only very rarely has a public REIT gone into bankruptcy.

We'll look next at the REIT balance sheet structure and how this relates to their ability to pay preferred dividends.

CHAPTER 5
What Is Preferred Stock?

A market analyst is an expert who will know tomorrow why the things he predicted yesterday didn't happen today!

Preferred shares are strange animals, little understood and somewhat thinly traded. They have some of the characteristics of bonds and some of stocks.

Broadly, Preferreds represent what is known as 'mezzanine financing'; it is not as risky as common shares, nor as safe as debt, but is somewhere in between. Thus owners of preferred stock should expect investment returns somewhere between debt and equity.

Comparison with debt

Like bonds, Preferreds pay a fixed amount, but in the form of a dividend (as opposed to interest). Interest and dividends are very similar, with the main difference being that:

- Dividends in some cases are qualified for the lower 15% tax rate (but not in the case of REITs).
- Dividends are voted on by the Company's board of directors, and non-payment does not trigger a creditor default. Non-payment can trigger some other actions which offer some limited investor protection.

The prices of the preferred shares will vary based on prevailing market interest rates and the credit worthiness of the issuing company and except in extreme circumstances will not change in price based on the earnings of the Company. So, if interest rates rise, such as frequently happens in an inflationary economy, just as in the case of debt, preferred shares prices can fall precipitously. Unlike with common shares, there is no possibility that the dividend of a preferred stock will increase over and above the stated amount on the preferred, and the owner of a preferred share does not, as it were, own a piece of the action (an ownership position in a company that will grow in value along with the profits of the enterprise).

Similarly, if a rating agency such as Moody's lowers the credit rating on a company, the investor will raise the required risk premium, causing the price of the preferred stock to drop to reflect the perceived increase in credit risk, just as will happen to the pricing of the company's bonds. We'll discuss this more fully later.

Pricing of Preferreds should be expected to be more volatile than debt: in other words, theoretically movements in market interest rates will impact preferred share prices more than the price of bonds. According to Kenneth Winans, author of *Preferreds: Wall Street's Best-Kept Income Secret*, Preferred stocks are more volatile than bonds. This should not be surprising. Unlike for bonds, there is no defined maturity date for Preferreds, making the interest rate part of the pricing risk much greater. Further, Preferreds are riskier than debt, since they are behind bonds in liquidation, so if credit changes for the worse or better, this will most likely cause a more significant price adjustment. However, in the case of a small group of non-investment grade REIT Preferreds, we learned that their prices are very highly correlated to below-investment grade bonds.

All the REIT preferred stocks discussed here are sold on the New York Stock Exchange, with transparency of mark-ups and volume, and are sold in $25 denominations. Debt remains opaque, and is sold in large denominations. So, while the preferred market is often 'thin' (low volume), it is by no means as imperfect as the bond market.

Like common stock, almost all REIT Preferreds pay their dividends quarterly (most bonds pay semi-annually).

Comparison with Common Stock

A preferred shareholder generally does not participate in the growth of the issuing Company's earnings (except through an improvement in the issuing Company's credit worthiness, which will cause a decline in the investors' risk premium). Dividend income paid at the current level is all a preferred investor can expect to receive, as opposed to a common stock investor who is hoping for both growing dividends plus price appreciation over a period of time.

With a little effort, savvy investors can find preferred shares that they expect to appreciate in price because of an improvement in the credit ranking of the issuer. This should generally be regarded as something extra, not the main reason for investing in the preferred.

Like common shares, preferred dividend payments are voted on by the Company's board of directors prior to each distribution, and there is no corporate penalty if preferred dividends are skipped. In the case of debt, if a REIT misses an interest payment on a mortgage it usually will trigger a default clause in the loan agreement which has to be cured within a limited time-frame (often as short as 30 days). Failure to cure can cause the bankruptcy of the REIT, and/or a loss of the secured asset to the lender. In the case of preferred stock, a failure to make a preferred dividend payment has much less drastic consequences. The Company continues to operate almost as normal.

Debt holders are paid interest, but preferred and common stockholders are paid dividends: as mentioned earlier, dividends generally don't have to be paid (although in the case of REITs, there are tax consequences if at least some distributions aren't made, which we'll discuss when we discuss the taxation of REIT dividends). Dividends on REIT Preferred stock are taxed similarly to interest on debt. Common stock offers a greater opportunity for long-term price appreciation which is taxed at capital gains rates, as opposed to debt and REIT preferred dividends which are taxed at ordinary income rates. We'll review this in more detail below.

In many cases, a company's debt is secured by a lien on the financed assets. Thus, in liquidation or bankruptcy, the debt holder has a good chance of some principal recovery. Some companies have an 'investment grade rating': a rating agency (such as Moody's or

Standard & Poor's) has rated their debt as investment grade, meaning that it is relatively secure. For these companies, their debt is mostly a general obligation of the company, but in liquidation the debt still sits ahead of preferred, just as the preferred stock is ahead of the common stock.

However there are safety provisions for preferred shareholders. Most (but not all) preferred shares are classified as 'cumulative': any unpaid preferred dividends 'cumulate' and assuming that the issuing Company's balance sheet recovers, the only loss to a preferred shareholder is the time value of money on the unpaid dividend. Of course, the act of not paying a preferred dividend will cause the market price of the preferred stock to drop precipitously as long as the dividend is perceived to be at risk, and this should cause a preferred shareholder to be concerned about principal protection. All the REIT preferred prospectuses that I have seen contain a provision that prevents a company from making distributions to common shareholders if a preferred dividend is missed. Thus, preferred dividends must be caught up and paid before distributions are made to common shareholders. Note that in the case of REITs there is an exception that permits some distributions to shareholders sufficient for the REIT to maintain its status with the IRS as a REIT. We have seen many REITs in the 2008-10 financial market crisis and economic slowdown cease paying cash *common* dividends to their ordinary shareholders while continuing to pay cash *preferred* dividends to their preferred shareholders. In contrast to Common Dividends, only two publicly traded REITs that I know of missed paying preferred dividends during the troubled period beginning in the fall of 2008, and since the REITs stayed in business, the dividends may well be caught up at a future date.

A further protection that is generally provided is that after preferred dividends are missed (generally six dividends, representing six quarters) the preferred shareholders as a class can elect two directors to represent them on the issuer's board of directors. This is a requirement of the NYSE, so you will find most preferred issues contain this protective backstop for preferred shareholders.

In liquidation, preferred shareholders are ahead of common share-holders, and most preferred shares have a stated liquidation value of

$25 per share, regardless of the initial purchase price. Thus, there is some chance that value can be realized from preferred shares even in liquidation. Practically, there have so far been almost no liquidations of publicly traded REITs.

Preferreds – "call" feature

Unlike debt which has a maturity date, preferred shares are like common stock; they are 'perpetual' and have no maturity date. Once you buy them, you own them forever (unless you sell them on the stock market) or UNLESS the issuer – the company – decides to 'call' the shares. In this event, the issuer publicly announces that it will redeem the preferred shares on a certain date, and the stock holder is required to surrender the shares at the stated call price (typically $25/share) plus accrued dividends.

For the first five years following the date of issuance, most preferred shares cannot be called. At any time thereafter, the issuer can call the preferred shares at the price that is in the issuing prospectus (generally $25 per share).

In effect the call provision is an option which is tremendously valuable to the issuer: after the first five years, the issuer can refinance the preferred whenever it chooses: when interest rates have declined, and money is flowing, the preferred investment can in effect be repurchased by the issuing company, and the investor is stuck looking around for an attractive investment alternative. Investors need to consider this embedded call option in their valuation of the preferred security.

Historic Performance of Preferreds

In his thorough analysis of Preferreds, *(Preferreds, Wall Street's Best-Kept Income Secret)* Kenneth Winans has some interesting statistics comparing different types of investment vehicles.

Preferred Stocks have returned an average of 7.3% a year (5% a year after inflation, excluding the war-time eras). This includes all kinds of Preferreds, including REITs, and represents a composite of the Mitchell Preferred Stock Average (1890 – 929), S&P (1929 – 1980) and the Winans International Preferred Stock Index (1980 – 2007).

REIT Preferreds have been around for a much shorter time, and in their current form, REITs with preferred shares outstanding have existed only since early 1995. During the period from early 2005 to early 2010, their average yield has approximated 8.3%.

Common Stocks have returned an average of 11.4% over almost the same time period. However their average annual dividend has been 4.5% versus 6.4% for preferred stocks.

Corporate Bonds have averaged an annual return of 5.8% (3.5% a year after inflation, excluding war-time eras) from 1900 – 2007. The average annual interest yield has been 5.7%.

Municipal Bonds have averaged a tax-free yield of 4.6% from 1900 – 2007. Adjusting this for the highest tax bracket, this equates to a pre-tax average yield of 6.2%, about 1% (100 bps) below preferred stocks' total return, but comparable to the average yield of preferred (6.4%).

REIT Preferreds: Performance

Since February 1995, the average REIT Preferred yield has varied from a low of 5.75% in March 2004 to a high of 15.7% in November 2008, with an average yield of 8.3%. The average yield for the past five years has been 8.1%, and as of December 2010 is 7.3%.

The period when the financial markets almost melted down, September of 2008 through May 2009, was when yields really spiked, and was abnormal for most asset classes. Excluding these periods and four exceptionally low-rate months in 2003-04, the average REIT Preferred yield has been between a low of 6.1% in June 2003 and a high of 10.95% in March 2000, with an average of 8.1%.

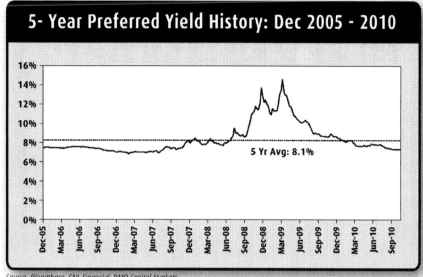

5- Year Preferred Yield History: Dec 2005 - 2010

5 Yr Avg: 8.1%

Source: Bloomberg, SNL Financial, BMO Capital Markets
Chart 6

While the pricing volatility that exists with REIT Preferreds is a cause for investor concern, it can be seen that over the long haul, REIT Preferreds have traded within a reasonable band. Since prices are the inverse of yield, there have been a few periods of time when REIT Preferred prices have fluctuated significantly. Through dollar cost averaging and some of the strategies outlined below, risks can be partially mitigated, and for the income investor who is more interested in an annuity, fluctuations in value are not fun, but not necessarily causes for alarm in a diverse portfolio. The fact that REIT securities are backed by hard assets and that REIT Preferreds generally have only a limited amount of debt ahead of them on the balance sheet gives comfort about principal valuation over the long run.

Convertible Preferreds

Some preferred shares are convertible into common shares at a pre-set price. Convertible Preferreds are a little more complicated to value and involve different underwriting than regular (non-convertible) Preferreds. While convertible Preferreds certainly can be sound investments, I have chosen to limit my investments to 'regular' Preferreds and have excluded them from this review.

CHAPTER 6

Real Estate Investment Trusts: Capitalization

Landlords grow rich in their sleep without working,
risking or economising.
– John Stuart Mill - *English Philosopher and Economist*

Compared to the $350 billion in REIT common equity that is outstanding, REIT Preferred stock has a market value of under $20 billion. So, REIT Preferreds are generally too small to be of interest to institutions and equity analysts, and thus can offer some real value in comparison with other more widely traded and bigger classes of public securities. Owners of REIT Preferreds tend not to trade them; together with the small size of each issue, this compounds the lack of liquidity, and thus puts them out of favor with major investors.

For instance, there is only one dedicated mutual fund and no dedicated ETFs that offers investors the chance to invest in a pool of REIT Preferreds. Investor interest in Preferreds (as a whole) is limited. Some REIT Preferreds are owned by income-oriented funds, but again, this is generally not the case. The reason for this is the lack of liquidity: it is hard for an institutional investor to build a position in any one stock.

On average, excluding mortgage REITs, REITs maintain about 50% of their capitalization as equity, and the remainder as debt, representing very low leverage compared to most private investors. REITs today are much less leveraged than they were prior to the early 90s. Just over half have some preferred equity, and for these, preferred stock typically represents 5% - 6% of their total capitalization.

	Total REITs*	Total REITs with Preferred	$ millions Tot Pref. Market Value
Healthcare	12	5	830
Office	16	10	2,887
Industrial	6	4	1,593
Office-Industrial	8	4	1,637
Shopping Center	13	9	2,280
Malls	8	4	883
Student Housing	2	-	
Manufactured Housing	3	-	
Multifamily	14	5	1,287
Self-Storage	4	1	3,343
Lodging	11	8	1,763
Specialty/Triple Net	14	4	1,092
Total	11	58	17,595

*Excludes Mortgage REITs Source: BMO

Chart 7

Although preferred stock is in a separate class, it is sometimes grouped with equity and sometimes with debt. Preferred sits 'behind' debt, which means that in liquidation, holders of debt are paid before preferred shareholders; owners of common shares are paid last. See Chart 8 for an example of the capital structure of a typical REIT with preferred stock.

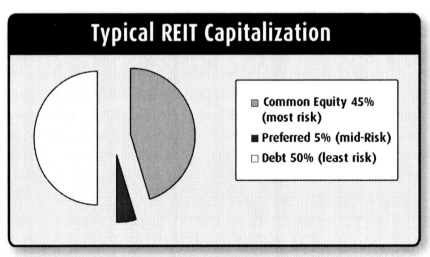

Chart 8

On the website of the National Association of Real Estate Investment Trusts (www.NAREIT.com) you'll find a more complete review of the REIT structure: there are some important facts to understand for investors who are concerned about default risks, or those wanting a more in-depth understanding.

CHAPTER 7

REITs: Property Types

*A property manager of an apartment community was showing
a unit to prospective residents and asking the usual questions:
"Do you have children?" the manager asked.
"Yes, nine and twelve," the wife answered.
"Animals?"
"Oh, no," she said earnestly. "They're very well behaved."*

REITs: investment categories

The 110+ equity REITs tend to specialize in one or two property types:
for instance a REIT may focus on apartments, or office, or even specific
office types (suburban or office buildings designed for specific tenant
types).

Publicly Traded Equity REITs		
Equity REITs *	$millions Total Equity Capitalization	Total Companies
Healthcare	40,200	12
Office	60,800	16
Industrial	16,200	6
Office-Industrial	16,700	8
Shopping Center	27,200	13
Malls	67,800	8
Student Housing	2,600	2
Manufactured Housing	2,800	3
Multifamily	51,200	14
Self-Storage	20,100	4
Lodging	21,400	11
Specialty/Triple Net	23,000	14
Total	350,000	111

*Excludes Mortgage REITs   Source: BMO
Chart 9

Individual REITs often focus on one geographic area or state (such as California, New York, Washington, DC, the Southeast). Almost all public REITs are now "internally managed" with the exception of hotel REITs, whose short rental period prevents them from qualifying as a REIT under the IRS regulations. The internally managed structure, whereby REIT management operates its properties, is generally much preferred by investors over the alternative of having a third-party management company manage the assets, which presents structural conflicts of interest.

Mortgage REITs

Mortgage REITs are very different from Equity REITs: they are in the business of lending money to real estate companies and partnerships, not operating the real estate. Their risks need to be evaluated differently to equity REITs and investment decisions modified accordingly. In particular, their debt financing options are far less clear-cut than for Equity REITs.

Although it is possible to make some good returns investing in Mortgage REITs as their fortunes ebb and flow, the author does not have the expertise to make sound investment decisions in these companies.

CHAPTER 8

Profits, Dividends, and Tax

There are just three types of accountants:
Those who can count and those who can't.

REITs: FFO and AFFO

For the past 20 years, the primary measure of performance for REITs has been Funds from Operations (FFO), as opposed to Net Income which is more regularly used for non-REITs (C Corporations). In simple terms, FFO is net income plus depreciation of real assets, or a quasi-'cash flow' before capital expenditures. Importantly, excluded from this measure are profits from the sale of properties as well as various other items that are 'adds' or 'deducts' from net income, which enables some investors to use FFO as a short-cut tool to evaluate the ability of a REIT to pay its dividends over a long-term period.

Over time regulatory bodies (namely: the SEC) have become involved in the definition of FFO. This was to tame the more creative interpretation of the term by a few REITs, and because FFO is not a measure under Generally Accepted Accounting Principles (GAAP) it still lacks the more disciplined definition of net income. Unfortunately, SEC rules have defined FFO into becoming a less useful measure than it once was, and so REITs and analysts will often use additional performance measures with additions or deductions from FFO. These will always be explained in footnotes in the financial disclosures of a REIT's financial reports.

CASH IS KING

Adjusted Funds from Operations (AFFO) represents FFO less capital expenditures required to maintain a property in an as-is state (sometimes referred to as 'recurring' capital expenditures). A REIT also incurs 'revenue-enhancing' capital expenditures, which are in addition to 'recurring' capital expenditures, and are categorized separately since they are designed to do something other than maintain the status quo. Assuming that debt remains constant, AFFO should be a reasonable measure of internally-generated cash flow which is free and clear and available to distribute to shareholders. Practically, however, there are the same adjustments for FFO that need to be made to AFFO to obtain a more serviceable performance measure.

Example of 'FFO' & 'AFFO' calculation

Net Income (as reported)	100
Income from Sale of Assets	-15
Real Estate Depreciation	30
Funds From Operations (FFO)	115
Recurring Capital Expenditures	-20
Adjusted Funds From Operations (AFFO)	95
Dividend	-70
Cash available after Dividend*	25

*to fund other Capital Expenditures

Chart 10

Unless a REIT has a lot of asset sales in a given year, FFO will always be a much bigger number than net income. Remember that a REIT has to distribute 90% of its net income in order to maintain its REIT status, but most REITs are distributing substantially more than this. In gauging the relative safety of an investment in a REIT (including in the preferred stock) it is useful to compare the common stock dividend to FFO and AFFO, reckoning that an unusually high payout ratio of either FFO or AFFO may become a trigger for some kind of event, potentially impacting the credit of the issuer. For the buyer of the preferred stock, this can present an opportunity, but it does introduce an element of risk.

REITs: Taxation

Dividends paid by REITs are taxable at ordinary income rates; they do not qualify for the favorable (lower) rates of non-REITs (C Corporations). This is because REITs are 'pass-through' entities (like a partnership), paying no federal corporate tax at the corporate level. However, because almost all REITs usually distribute more than their net income, part of the common dividend is usually not currently taxable, and classed as 'return of capital.'

For instance, REIT 'A' with a common dividend of $1.00 may have 30%, or 30 cents classified as return of capital. This will not be taxed in the year of distribution but will reduce the investor's basis in the share. Obviously, this is highly attractive to the investor, and can reduce the current tax rate payable on common dividends quite significantly (for instance, the current taxable income can be as low as 50% on the distributions of some REITs). So, if an investor buys the share for $20.00/share, after the first year the investor's basis is reduced by 30 cents, to $19.70 per share. In a subsequent sale of the stock, the reduced basis increases the amount of capital gain paid by the investor.

In practice, unlike REIT common shares, distributions made on REIT Preferred shares are usually 100% taxable at ordinary income rates, which is similar to the treatment on interest income. From time to time, some REITs will report part of the preferred dividends to be return of capital or capital gain, thereby reducing the current tax burden of the investor. Because of the high current level of tax, REIT Preferred shares are usually best held in tax-advantaged accounts, such as a 401(k), 403(b), or IRA.

Tennessee, which has an income tax on unearned income, offers tax relief on some REIT dividends, which can make owning REITs and REIT Preferreds in taxable accounts more attractive. I am not aware of this in other states, but it is certainly worth checking your local state tax code.

CHAPTER 9

REIT Preferreds: Dividend Yields

If you're given a choice between cash and sex appeal, take the cash. As you get older, the cash will become your sex appeal!

REIT Preferred pricing and yields

Almost all REIT Preferreds are issued at $25 per share; carry a 'liquidation preference' of $25, and a call price of $25.

This means that upon original issuance, the dividend yield is set so that the shares will be successfully sold to the general public at $25 per share. The net proceeds to the Company will be less than that, as there will be brokerage and legal costs that may represent up to 4% of the total. Bear in mind that the issuing REIT will frequently have priced the preferred at what it judges to be the optimum time (when the yield will be lowest and the price will be highest): in other words, $25 may represent a high price, but not necessarily a fair price for the security over an extended period of time. Of course, this is not necessarily always the case, since REITs will issue securities to meet funding obligations (and since REITs retain little or no cash, they have to use external funding sources much more frequently than non-REITs).

The liquidation preference which is typically $25/share represents the amount that the preferred shareholder will be paid if the Company is liquidated, assuming that there are funds available after the lenders have been paid (lenders hold a senior position to the preferred share holders). Under most circumstances, this should be of academic interest, only.

The call date and the call price are key pieces of information. As mentioned above, almost all regular (excluding convertibles) REIT Preferred shares may be called after five years for the liquidation price, generally at $25 per share. If the stock is called, the investor is compelled to tender the shares for the call price ($25). So, you can see that this can become very important, depending on:

1. If the preferred stock has been issued for less than five years most REIT Preferreds cannot be called.
2. If the preferred stock is trading below $25, it is unlikely to be called. This is because it doesn't make sense to refinance it with another preferred stock series. However, it may make sense to refinance it with common equity or debt, so a call can occasionally be made.
3. Conversely, preferred issues that have been around for longer than five years and which trade above $25 are vulnerable to be 'called,' especially triggered by a drop in long-term interest rates. Hence the measure 'yield to call' becomes very important: this represents the yield on the stock assuming that the stock is called at the first available opportunity.
4. Another related measure is the 'yield to worst,' which assumes that the preferred is called at the least favorable time, which is not necessarily the first available opportunity.
5. Picking stocks which sell below $25 becomes relatively easy, as the 'yield to call' and 'yield to worst' measures can be disregarded. As a practical matter, I have never invested in stocks that are trading above the call price, although from time to time I have found myself in a position where the stock trades up above $25. In most cases I then plan my exit strategy after one year (as soon as the profit on the sale can be treated as a capital gain).

'Yield,' 'Yield to Call' and 'Yield to Worst': Calculations

As mentioned above, 'Yield to Call' assumes that the issuer exercises its right to call the stock at the first opportunity. 'Yield to Worst' assumes that the least favorable set of circumstances to the investor occurs. 'Yield' is simply the annualized dividend divided by the current price.

Example 1: Assume Preferred Stock 'A' is trading at above its call price, say $25.25 per share. The stock was issued in April 2010, pays a quarterly dividend of $0.50, and has a liquidation (and call) price of $25. The first call date will be April 2015.

The 'Yield' Calculation assumes cash flows as follows:

Purchase Price: $25.25

Annualized Dividend: $2.00

Yield: 7.9%

The 'Yield to Call' calculation assumes cash flows as follows:

Purchase price: $25.25

Call Date: April 2015

Call Price: $25

Dividends through April 2015

Yield to Call: 7.75%

The 'Yield to Worst' calculation in this case is identical to the 'Yield to Call.' This is because the worst possible scenario (other than issuer default!) is that the issuer calls the stock at the earliest opportunity.

Example 2: Assume Preferred Stock 'B' is trading at below its call price, say $24.50 per share. The stock was issued in April 2005 and thus became callable in April 2010. 30 days' notice is required to call the stock. Preferred 'B' pays a quarterly dividend of $0.50 and has a liquidation (and call) price of $25.

The 'Yield' Calculation assumes cash flows as follows:

Purchase Price: $24.50

Annualized Dividend: $2.00

Yield: 8.2%

The 'Yield to Call' calculation for Example 2 assumes as follows:

Purchase price: $24.50

Last Ex-Dividend date: Yesterday

Call Date: 30 days from now

Call Price: $25

Dividends through: next 30 days

Yield to Call: The investor pays $24.50, receives one month's dividend ($0.17), plus the call price $25 for a total return of $0.67 on a $24.50 investment which is 2.7%, or 33% annualized!

The 'Yield to Worst' calculation for Example 2 case assumes as follows:

Purchase price: $24.50
Call Date: Never
Call Price: N/A
Dividends through: Continue to be paid quarterly
Yield to Worst: 8.2% (same as Yield)

Strip Yield: Calculations

The Strip Yield takes into account the timing of the next dividend to calculate the yield. For instance, suppose a stock is trading for $25/share and has a quarterly dividend of $0.50, a yield of 8%. Let's suppose you buy the stock on the day before the stock goes 'ex-dividend.' In that case you get one quarterly dividend 'free,' so you should deduct this one quarter's dividend from the purchase price of the stock. So, the Strip Yield is $2/($25-$0.50) = $2.00/$24.50 = 8.2%.

Strip yields are helpful in making careful comparisons between preferred stocks to determine the fair price of the shares.

CHAPTER 10

Credit and Credit Ratings: Why Credit Rating Agencies Under-rate REITs

Why do credit analysts get excited on Saturdays?
They can wear casual clothes to work.

Credit quality

The primary driver of REIT Preferred share prices is interest rates, which is made up of two components:

1. US Treasury Bond yields
2. Credit Spreads: The financial risks associated with a specific issuer (the issuer's 'risk premium') and associated with investing in debt other than US Treasuries

REIT Preferred share prices are impacted by changes in the above, and are not directly affected by Company earnings: Unlike common shares, preferred shares don't participate directly in the earnings of a company.

Changes in the perceived or actual financial strength of a REIT can occur in several ways. For instance, an individual issuer can show market strength or weakness in its quarterly results, rental pricing may change, and thereby change the issuer's perceived ability to pay the preferred dividends. Or a significant acquisition financed mainly with debt will give the Rating Agencies cause to lower the credit rating of the acquirer.

The Rating Agencies rate many preferred issuers and their securities. The best-known and largest two credit rating agencies are Moody's and Standard & Poor's. They each rate preferred stock, and investors then classify the securities into two buckets, 'Investment Grade' and 'Non-Investment Grade.'

Rating Description	Moody's	Standard & Poor's
Investment Grade	Aaa	AAA
	Aa1	AA+
	Aa2	AA
	Aa3	AA-
	A1	A+
	A2	A
	A3	A-
	Baa1	BBB+
	Baa2	BBB
	Baa3	BBB-
Non-Investment Grade	Ba1	BB+
	Ba2	BB
	Ba3	BB-
	B1/B2/B3	B+/B/B-

Chart 11

The Rating Agencies have both objective and subjective criteria for evaluating the credit of a REIT. These include the amount of secured debt on the balance sheet, total leverage, fixed charge coverage, and other measures of their view of a REIT's ability to withstand a financial or economic downturn.

The rating process

Rating Agencies have two primary concerns to evaluate:

1. The risk of an issuer's default and
2. The likelihood of recovery of principal in bankruptcy.

Rating Agencies correctly judge that the risk of default of REITs with leverage in compliance with unsecured bond covenants is extremely low, so on this criterion, there is little reason to judge preferred stock to be more risky than senior unsecured debt.

However, in the case of bankruptcy, senior debt comes ahead of preferred stock: in other words, owners of bonds are paid before owners of preferred stock. So preferred stock is in this theoretical case more risky than senior debt, and as a result is rated below senior debt.

In the case of Moody's, for investment grade REITs, they rate their preferred stock one notch below senior debt. Standard & Poor's takes a more conservative approach: for investment grade REITs, S&P rates preferred stock two notches below senior debt. This is because they believe that the legal structure of REITs, with most assets held in a subsidiary entity, increases the recovery risk to preferred shareholders in bankruptcy.

Why does the credit rating matter?

REITs borrow money in two primary ways: they either issue corporate debt or borrow mortgage debt. Corporate debt is unsecured, which is purchased by lenders based on the credit of the issuing company. Mortgage debt is secured, and is attached to (secured by) a mortgage on an individual property (or group of properties). Companies that are listed as 'investment grade' have much greater ability to access the unsecured debt markets: lenders rely on the investment grade rating from the major rating agencies as a seal of approval.

Having an investment grade rating increases the number of debt sources that can be accessed by a REIT, and reduces its debt refinancing risk. Rating Agencies have to carefully develop and evaluate various criteria that will impact a REIT's ability to continue to operate in a financially sound manner, and ultimately be able to repay its debt.

In a similar manner, Rating Agencies rate particular preferred series, relying on the data that they collect on the Company, and assess the ability of the REIT to pay the dividends on the Preferred continuously. Buyers of investment grade Preferreds can similarly be reasonably comforted by the fact that one or more expert third parties have applied a rational process to evaluate the credit quality of the preferred.

Why Rating Agencies are too conservative in their evaluations of REITs

Of the 111 REITs listed in a recent KeyBanc Report, only 9 have senior unsecured debt ratings of BBB+ (Moody's Baa1) or above. Only 41 have senior unsecured debt that is rated as investment grade, BBB- (Moody's Baa3) or above.

There are several reasons why the Rating Agencies tend to under-rate REITs. Perhaps the first is the relative novelty of post-1993 REITs. Up until then there were not only few public real estate companies, but also few that were structured as REITs with all the related limitations and complexities. REITs' track record at dealing with economic cycles is still perhaps less tested than other industries and corporate structures. The Rating Agencies also tend to penalize REITs in their ratings because REIT structures tend to be relatively complex: as described in the section on REITs above, many REITs are organized with an UPREIT (Umbrella Partnership) as a subsidiary entity 'below' the publicly-traded REIT, which owns most of the assets, and which in theory could present some impediment to debt or preferred holders in bankruptcy. REITs also have other characteristics that concern the Rating Agencies, including the capital intensity of the real estate ownership business, their dividend-paying requirements, and both IRS and sometimes contractual impediments to selling assets. All of these factors contribute to what may theoretically seem risky to lenders and rating agencies, but experience under arguably the toughest of circumstances in 2008-09 has shown to be reasonably manageable.

As a result of this, both senior debt ratings and preferred stock ratings of REITs tend to be too low. The proof of this has been the extremely low default rate of public non-mortgage REITs since 1993, and the remarkable strength shown by REITs during the severe recession and financial crisis of 2008-09. During this period credit losses by REIT lenders and by public preferred and common shareholders have been minimal. The only public REIT that has gone into bankruptcy since 1993 that I'm aware of is General Growth Properties, which was indeed highly leveraged with a big development pipeline that ran onto the rocks during the economic and financial crisis of 2009.

To my knowledge, there were only three public non-mortgage REITs (Strategic Hotels, Felcor Lodging Trust, and MPG Office Trust) that suspended preferred dividends effective in 2009, all highly leveraged REITs with risky strategies. Felcor subsequently reinstated its preferred dividend after seven missed quarters.

When rating both a REIT's senior unsecured debt and preferred stock, Rating Agencies penalize a REIT for using secured debt. They believe that the existence of secured debt on a REIT's balance sheet impedes its access to capital. There is little reason why the preferred stock is more risky if it is issued by a REIT that exclusively uses secured debt than if it uses unsecured debt, assuming that other ratios are the same. The unsecured borrower may arguably have tighter loan covenants, but there is nothing to stop an unsecured borrower from paying off the unsecured debt, as indeed some companies have done. The traditional argument is undeniable that in a financial melt-down, a company using unsecured debt has more options than a user of secured debt (the unsecured debt user can take on secured debt in a crisis, but not vice versa). However, unsecured borrowers are subject to covenant limitations about the amount of secured debt that they can take on, and since the unsecured market was effectively shut down for much of the financial crisis of 2009, the crisis was at least as much of a financing problem for unsecured borrowers as for secured borrowers.

We also found that public REITs tend to be the most attractive borrowing candidates for secured lenders, especially in troubled times: they are generally professionally run, with solid corporate governance, and significantly lower leverage than most private secured borrowers. Thus while debt capital may be in short supply in a financial crisis, REITs are the most likely to find availability of secured debt. It is far from clear that preferred stock issued by secured borrowers is more risky than preferred stock issued by unsecured borrowers. Other factors, especially overall leverage, are far more relevant.

As a result, while it is clearly a subject for debate, in my view the Rating Agencies have been overly conservative in evaluating credit risk for REITs, and this is particularly the case in rating REIT preferred stock. There are also difficult issues for the Rating Agencies in fully understanding the impact of differing investment strategies, for instance, the differing types of development (the risky large, multi-use urban development compared to much less risky small suburban development). REITs with development of any magnitude are much more exposed to a credit problem than REITs without development, and perhaps the Rating Agency models do not weight this difference adequately.

We see that there are 57 REITs with preferred stock outstanding, but only 14 of these have an investment grade rating or a 'split rating' (investment grade from one of the two major rating agencies, but non-investment grade from the other) on their preferred stock, while a further 11 have investment grade ratings on their senior debt but not their preferred stock:

- The preferred stock of the 14 REITs with Preferreds that are rated as investment grade at the time of writing have an average yield of 6.9%.
- Of the 11 REITs whose senior debt is rated investment grade, but whose preferred stock is rated below investment grade (and thus is judged by the Rating Agencies to be 'speculative'), the average yield at the time of writing is 7.1%.
- The remaining 30 non-Mortgage REITs with ratings that are below investment grade or are not rated have preferred shares outstanding with an average yield at the time of writing of 8.1%, and it is this group that presents the greatest opportunity. While all the REITs are rated unfavorably, it is the non-rated and below investment grade that are penalized the most heavily by REIT Preferred investors.

| | Total REITs with Preferred | | |
| | with Preferred | Investment Grade | |
		Corporate	Preferred
Healthcare	4		1
Office	10	4	2
Industrial	5	2	2
Office-Industrial	4	2	
Shopping Center	9	3	2
Malls	4	1	1
Student Housing	–		
Manufactured Housing	–		
Multifamily	7	4	3
Self-Storage	1	1	1
Lodging	8	1	
Specialty/Triple Net	5	1	1
Total	57	19	13

Excludes Mortgage REITs   Sources: BMO 7-20-10, Key Banc 7-16-10

Chart 12

I'll later describe how you can use this information to make smart investment decisions.

CHAPTER 11

Interest Rates and Preferred Stock Pricing

Q: What is Ben Bernanke's favorite PC game?
A: Roller Coaster Tycoon

Interest Rates

As discussed, there are two components of interest rates, Treasury Bond yields (perhaps most relevantly the 10-year Treasury Bond, which is widely followed), and 'credit spreads' (which represent the risk and liquidity premiums investors require for putting their money into something other than 'risk-free' Treasuries).

Preferred stock is often perceived to carry little price risk. In other words, when buying a preferred stock, many unsophisticated investors believe that they are pretty sure of getting back their principal, plus the dividends that have been paid during the holding period. Nothing could be further from the truth. Preferred stock pricing can be volatile, and investors are by no means assured of protecting their principal, so it is important to understand why.

The most important fact is that preferred stock has no maturity date. While the issuer may use its prerogative to 'call' the stock when it suits it, the owner (buyer) of the stock has no similar opportunity: in other words, the issuer has a free 'call' opportunity, but the owner of the preferred does not have a free 'put' opportunity. The issuer will usually call the preferred when:

1. The preferred can be re-issued at a lower rate, or
2. The preferred can be refinanced with common stock, or a combination of debt and common stock, at a lower overall rate.

CASH IS KING

It is quite likely that a particular preferred stock may remain on the market, uncalled, for a very long time, and since the investor has no such 'put' rights has to rely on the operation of the market if he needs to sell the stock.

So, the math is quite straightforward: the investor is locked into receiving a fixed dividend payment forever unless he sells the stock. If investors' required rate of return for a preferred stock of REIT A is 8%, given a $2 dividend/year, the stock will trade at $25. It is fairly easy to see that if investors' required rate of return changes to 10%, since the dividend is still $2, the price of REIT A's preferred stock will drop; dividing $2 by 10% gives the new price of $20.

In order to address price fluctuations in preferred stock prices, it is helpful to invest over a period of time, and to reinvest the dividends in REIT Preferreds to dollar-cost average.

Treasuries

For the last 20 years, interest rates on Treasuries have been on a downward trend. Owners of fixed rate investments such as preferred stock have had this tremendous advantage, since price moves with the inverse of yield. As an example, the direction of 10-year Treasuries will likely have some bearing on the price performance of preferreds: if I bought a $25 preferred when 10-year Treasuries were 6%, the stock will likely be worth more if the yield on 10-year Treasuries drops to 3%. Treasury rates reached a new low of 2.40% in early October 2010, but rose sharply in early December, reaching 3.45%.

The following chart shows historic rates on the 10-year Treasury. It is easy to see that rates may return to what appears to be a more sustainable long-term level in the 5% range, compared to the 3% range where rates have been recently. Loose monetary policies as currently being practiced by the Government and the Federal Reserve could lead to a future bout of inflation, in which case 10-year Treasuries could rise above this level at some future time. The Fed's intervention in the capital markets, including actively buying mortgage bonds, is designed to bring down mortgage rates, which are directly tied to the 10-year Treasury rates. Until the announcement of a second round of 'Quantitative Easing' in December 2010, the Fed's policy arguably reduced the rate on the 10-year Treasury Bond by about 0.5%, but the news of the second round had the opposite effect than intended, raised the specter of inflation, and long-term interest rates jumped 100 basis points (bps) or 1%.

An investor would then need to consider: if the rate on the 10-year Treasury bond rises to 5%, should he continue to own preferred stock yielding 8%, which was attractive when the 10-year Treasury was 3%? In most cases the answer is probably that he will demand a higher return, causing the price of the preferred stock to drop. However, it is interesting to note that in November and December 2010 the rate on 10-year Treasuries rose by 105 bps in 65 days; during that period the weighted average yield on the preferred stock universe followed by the analysts at Bank of Montreal remained at 7.3%. Credit spreads contracted during this time period to offset the increase in Treasury rates. We'll discuss why this occurred later in the chapter.

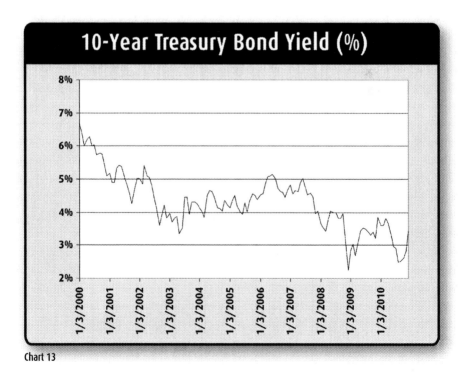

Chart 13

REIT Preferred stock: Credit Spreads

REIT Preferred stocks have typically traded at 2% - 4% (200 bps – 400 bps) above the 10-year Treasury, and, in the last 10 years, an average of 375 bps. This is the 'Credit Spread.' As can be seen in Chart 13, spreads briefly gapped out at over 1200 bps during the financial crisis of late 2008-09, but are returning to closer to normal now.

Spreads are impacted by two considerations:

- Credit risk: as we've seen, the credit rating has an impact on yield expectations. Especially for REIT issuers of preferred stock (few of which are investment grade), access to equity and debt capital is also important. There have been times when these credit markets have been closed to all but the most credit-worthy REITs.
- Overall return: investors will expand or contract their return expectations based on the array of alternative investments.

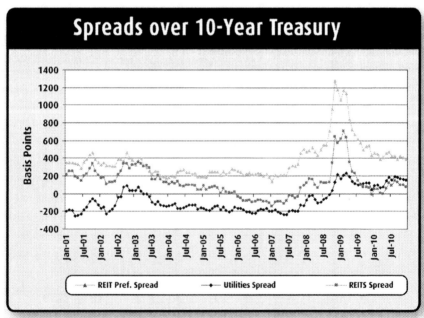

Source: Raymond James
Chart 14

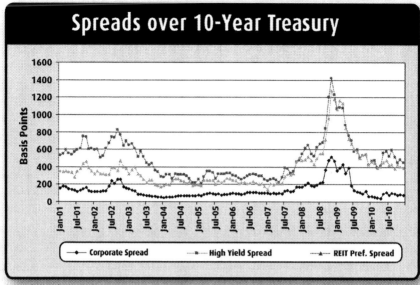

Spreads over 10-Year Treasury

Source: Raymond James
Chart 15

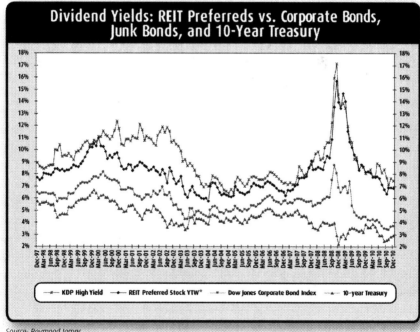

Dividend Yields: REIT Preferreds vs. Corporate Bonds, Junk Bonds, and 10-Year Treasury

Source: Raymond James
Chart 16

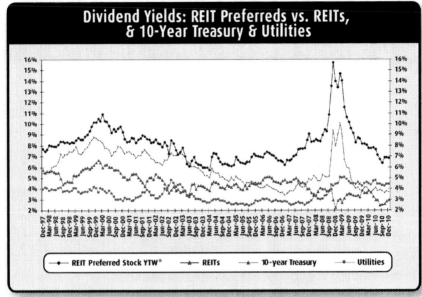

Dividend Yields: REIT Preferreds vs. REITs, & 10-Year Treasury & Utilities

Legend: REIT Preferred Stock YTW* — REITs — 10-year Treasury — Utilities

Source: Raymond James
Chart 17

Why REIT prices held firm in the latter part of 2010

The 1% (100 bps) increase in the 10-year Treasury bond yield between October and December 2010 was not matched by an increase in the yield on REIT Preferreds, which remained steady at 7.3%. In other words, Treasury prices fell significantly, and REIT Preferred prices remained firm. This seems to be intuitively inconsistent. However, as we'll see in the next chapter, REIT Preferred prices and the long-term Treasury bond are not highly correlated.

It is worth examining this to better understand the risks that the REIT Preferred investor faces from rising Treasury rates.

In the next chapter, we'll discuss the data that we've analyzed that shows over a 6-year period (2004 – 2010), the 20-year Treasury bond index has been negatively correlated with REIT Preferred prices, while the 10-year Treasury bond index has almost a zero correlation. The implication of this is that Treasuries can fluctuate but they don't impact REIT Preferred prices. This interesting finding needs to be tempered by the fact that this was a period of extreme interest rate fluctuations, especially for corporate debt that was below investment grade. Overall, interest rates on long-term Treasuries dropped throughout the 6-year period. During the 2008-09 time period, while Treasury rates continued to drop, credit spreads (especially for companies that were below investment grade) widened dramatically, driving REIT Preferred yields to extreme levels. So, we should not conclude that the low correlation for the past six years of Treasuries and REIT Preferreds will necessarily continue for the next six years!

There are several reasons why I believe investors did not demand a higher yield for REIT Preferreds during the October – December 2010 time period:

- REIT prices have been heading higher (yields have been dropping) for over a year. With the increase in Treasury yields, REIT Preferred prices stopped continuing to increase, but didn't drop.
- Treasuries in October 2010 were artificially low, caused by anticipation of Fed action to lower long-term interest rates ('QE2'). The action of the Fed in December to extend quantitative easing and of Congress to continue the low Bush-era tax rates had the unanticipated effect of increasing fears of inflation that caused 10-year Treasury rates to rise.
- In mid-October 2010, REIT Preferred credit spreads were effectively 4.9%. By mid-December 2010, credit spreads had contracted to 3.9%. The normal credit spread of REIT Preferreds over the 10-year Treasury is 3.7%. So there was room for the credit spread to contract, especially as the strength of the REITs' balance sheets and their business continued to improve.

2010	October	December
10 Year Treasury	2.4%	3.5%
Credit Spread	4.9%	3.9%
Total REIT Pref. Yield	7.3%	7.3%

Chart 18

CHAPTER 12

Major Investment Risks

*Ostriches are investors who stick to their old strategies,
oblivious to changes in the world around them.*

Interest Rate Risk

Apart from some unusual periods, for 15 years investor return
expectations for REIT Preferreds have been in the 6% - 9% range,
and have averaged 8.3%. Of course, an increase in investor return
expectations from 6% to 9% implies a massive 1/3 drop in preferred
stock valuation. It is quite within the realm of possibilities that
Treasuries yields can spike by 2% (200 basis points) in 2 years. It is
logical to think that a rise in Treasury yields (a reduction in Treasury
prices) will similarly trigger a reduction in preferred valuations. On
this basis, a 2% increase in Treasury yields could potentially trigger
a 20% reduction in value. In the example below relating to theoretical
preferred stock valuations, Treasuries rise by 2% (200 bps) over
three years. At the same time credit spreads compress because the
economy has improved, reducing issuers' risk of default. The 2%
Treasury increase less a 75 bps reduction in credit spreads causes
the preferred yield to rise from 7.25% to 8.5%. Since the preferred
dividend is constant (at $7.50 per preferred share in the example
below), the preferred share price must drop accordingly, by 15%:

	Treasury Yield	Risk Premium	Preferred Yield	Preferred Dividend	Preferred Price
Year 1	3.0%	4.25%	7.25%	$7.25	$100.00
Year 3	5.0%	3.50%	8.50%	$7.25	$85.29

Chart 19

It is very interesting to note that over the past 6 years there has been a low correlation between a basket of preferred stocks that I have owned and 10-year Treasury bond prices, and a negative correlation with 20-year Treasury bond prices. The meaning of this low/negative correlation is that over the past 6 years (through May 2010) preferred prices moved independently of Treasuries. The possible reasons for this are that:

1. During this time period the near-collapse of the credit markets caused a massive rally in Treasuries at the expense of all share prices, including prices of preferred stock. Credit spreads widened dramatically during the liquidity crisis causing REIT Preferred pricing to contract rapidly. This may be a "Black Swan" event that can mislead investors to thinking that rising long-term Treasury interest rates may not impact REIT Preferreds.
2. The basket of shares was skewed towards non-investment grade Preferreds, indicating that investors perceived them to be higher risk.

We hope under most circumstances that the example above may be a worst case, although during the credit crisis of 2008-09 we saw preferred stock yields more than double for a brief period, and as a result prices drop by more than 50% before recovering within 18 months. It is also likely that as we saw at the end of 2010, as Treasury yields rise credit spreads will compress, offsetting part of the increase and resulting in a less severe drop in price.

Dealing with interest rate risk is one of the biggest challenges of investing in REIT Preferred stocks, as rates have the potential to have such a big impact. With no maturity rate for their investments, owners of REIT Preferred stocks are very exposed to inflation and rising interest rates. Interest rates are notoriously difficult to forecast, and so managing this risk is difficult.

Keep this in mind as we pull together our investment strategy later.....

Hedging

Hedging is one strategy investors use to mitigate risk. In theory, the owner of a REIT Preferred stock should be willing to give up some of his return in order to protect himself against a run up in interest rates.

Investors in equities can do this easily through various strategies using options on market indices. Often a strategy can be developed which involves minimizing the cost through retaining some part of the risk. For instance, an equity investor may elect to buy a 'collar,' such as to give up one-year returns above 10% in exchange for protecting a loss of more than 10% by selling a 'call' option at 110, which offsets the cost of buying a 'put' option at 90.

In trying to develop a hedging strategy to mitigate exposure resulting from rising interest rates, one of the primary problems we face is that the market for REIT Preferred stock is small, and thus there are no exactly applicable derivatives that have been developed which can be used for hedging. However, we did find two indices, HYK (High Yield Corporate Bonds) and JNK (High Yield Bonds) that over the past three years have a very high correlation with a basket of 11 REIT Preferreds that I have owned over part of the period. Derivatives can be bought on both of these indices.

Correlation with 11 REIT Preferreds						
	HYG HIGH YIELD CORP BONDS	JNK HIGH YIELD BONDS	LQD INVESTMENT GRADE CORP BONDS	IYR US REAL ESTATE	TNX 10+ YEAR TREASURY	TLT 20+ YEAR TREASURY
Correlation	96%	98%	57%	59%	9%	-23%
# Months	37	38	72	72	72	72

Chart 20

*Portfolio	AIV-PU	BDN-PD	CBL-PC	CLP-PD	CUZ-PA	DDR-PI
	DRE-PJ	DRE-PN	FR-PJ	GRT-PG	PKY-PD	

Chart 21

The correlation with high yield bonds is not surprising, in that none of the selected Portfolio of REIT Preferreds is investment grade. The relatively short period examined (3-6 years) was necessitated by the short history of some of the preferred issues and the sum of the indices. During this short life there have been extreme fluctuations in prices of Preferreds, bonds and Treasuries, and during this time (late 2008 through early 2010) credit spreads for low grade bonds (and Preferreds) widened to levels never believed possible. High yield bonds and preferred yields reached record yield levels, and Treasury yields reached record lows. This must at least partially explain the lack of correlation between the pricing of Treasuries and Preferreds.

We explored the feasibility of hedging the preferred portfolio. Unfortunately it was possible only to 'short' the indices for periods of up to a year, and the cost was extremely high; this could reflect the expectation that prices are going to drop precipitously, or it could reflect a lack of liquidity. We determined that we needed to take an alternative approach to managing interest rate risk, which we have to address primarily through investment portfolio diversification and dollar cost averaging.

Dealing with what may be the biggest risk to REIT Preferred investors: 'Waldenization'

In February 2000 Walden Residential Properties was acquired through a leveraged buy-out by Olympus Real Estate Holdings. Both were Dallas-based companies; the difference was that Walden was a public company with common and preferred shares traded on the New York Stock Exchange. Olympus was a private company specializing in private leveraged real estate acquisitions, controlled by well-known buy-out firm Hicks, Muse, Tate, and Furst of New York. Hicks Muse specialized in acquiring companies using small amounts of equity and large quantities of debt.

After reputable investment banks began to sell unrated or below investment grade Preferreds in the mid-1990s, these Preferreds were widely believed to be safe investments even for 'widows and orphans' – shares that could be put away in the safety deposit box and forgotten about.

The shocker about the acquisition of Walden was that Olympus proposed to buy – and Walden's Board proposed to sell – Walden's common shares while leaving the preferred stock outstanding. The impact on Walden preferred shareholders was potentially devastating as Olympus clearly planned to add hundreds of millions of dollars of debt to the Walden balance sheet ahead of the preferred shareholders.

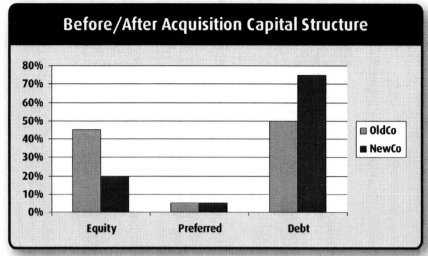

Before/After Acquisition Capital Structure

Chart 22

In a typical case of 'Waldenization,' in which the Public Company 'OldCo' is acquired by a New Private Company 'NewCo,' the preferred shareholder finds that the risk level of his investment has risen hugely. This happens when NewCo bids and acquires only the common shares of OldCo, leaving the preferred shares untouched. The credit quality of NewCo is much lower than OldCo, and in addition the preferred shares will likely be delisted from the New York Stock Exchange and become traded 'Over The Counter.' The preferred shares of OldCo thus become much less liquid, leaving OldCo preferred shareholders with a relatively worthless investment. The resulting collapse in the preferred share price causes a big capital loss for preferred shareholders, who often had mistakenly bought the shares thinking that they were buying a conservative investment.

In the case of Walden, after the announcement of the acquisition by Olympus, the Walden preferred share price did indeed collapse, but, as a result of a lawsuit, Olympus acquired all the preferred shares at a 20% discount to the call-price, with a resultant loss to the preferred shareolders, but not the devastating loss that they potentially faced.

There have been at least six cases of Waldenization where the acquisition of a REIT has been consummated by a private equity firm, and the preferred shares have been left outstanding, causing huge losses to the preferred shareholders. Perhaps most notoriously in the real estate bubble of 2007-08 several REITs were taken private at inflated prices just before the recession hit, and preferred stock investors lost large amounts of principal. In the case of Equity Inns, a Memphis-based hotel REIT, Equity Inns' Board approved a sale of its public common shares in 2008 to a Whitehall (Goldman Sachs) fund which left the preferred stock in place. The Equity Inns preferred was indeed de-listed from the NYSE, and became very illiquid. Within a short space of time, the holders of the debt of Equity Inns triggered default clauses in the debt covenants that caused Whitehall to cease paying the dividends on the Equity Inns preferred stock, completing the wipe-out of the preferred shareholders.

Why, you ask, would a Board of Directors of an acquired company approve a sale to a buyer that plans to destroy the investment of the preferred shareholders, in effect becoming complicit in this action? They receive legal advice that their fiduciary responsibility is to the common shareholders, not to the preferred shareholders or debt owners. Presumably, the legal advice is that they must maximize the price obtained by the common shareholder, in which case the preferred shareholder is being treated somewhat like a debt owner, and protected only to the extent that is required under the terms of the preferred prospectus.

Until recently, issuing companies have done little to protect the investor from the Waldenization risk, and indeed the hands of their Boards are somewhat tied. Designing a preferred stock that can be 'put' back to the issuer should the issuer's common shares no longer be traded on a major stock exchange does not pass the accounting rules: such a provision would require the preferred to be classified as debt, or at least as mezzanine financing, and not as equity, which would be a major problem for many issuers. And judging by the practice of the boards of directors of selling companies, directors must feel obligated to obtain the best sales price for the common shares regardless of what happens to the owners of the preferred stock.

Preferred stock, like all publicly traded securities, is described in a prospectus filed with the SEC, and is supposed to fully describe the investment risks. Despite efforts of the SEC to make the prospectus intelligible to the individual investor, understanding the risks that are disclosed in the prospectus is difficult. Prodded by their securities counsel, companies tend to discuss a litany of risks in their prospectus supplements, and it is hard to discriminate how many of the listed risks are real and how many are remote. The Waldenization risk is real.

Subsquent to the Walden shock, new non-investment grade preferred issues introduced a somewhat toothless provision which requires a step-up in the preferred dividend if the Company is acquired and the common stock de-listed, and the preferred shares remain outstanding. However, the step-up is only 1%, far less than fair compensation for the loss of credit quality.

Step-Ups and Dupont Fabros

In late 2010, in recognition of this risk, there was a move by underwriters to address this genuine investor concern. The first idea introduced was the insertion of a 4% step up in dividend yield for non-investment grade REIT Preferreds in the event of **both** a change of control and the de-listing (from the NYSE) of the preferred. Investment grade preferreds, which have a reduced risk of being Waldenized, will probably not contain this step-up provision. This was brought about by a few institutional investors seeking yield opportunities becoming interested in taking a position in non-rated REIT preferreds. These institutions had the market power to require greater protection against Waldenization.

The first REIT Preferred Series containing this improvement was a Series A preferred issued in October 2010 by Dupont Fabros Technology, Inc., a REIT that owns Data Centers.

Kite Realty

While this is a much-needed improvement, it was really insufficient protection, and a subsequent sale of a Series A preferred stock by Kite Realty provided for a 4% step up in dividend yield should there be **either** a change of control **or** a de-listing of the preferred. If this Kite format becomes an industry standard for non-investment grade preferreds it will begin to recompense investors for their loss of credit quality and (de facto) liquidity in an event of Waldenization. While it does not remove the fact that Waldenization dramatically changes the credit quality of the Preferred, it is at least likely that the value of the preferred will remain a lot closer to the call price than a REIT Preferred without this 4% step-up feature. As importantly, the acquiring company will give serious thought to redeeming the Preferred since its yield will not be as attractive to the acquirer as it once was.

Cogdell Spencer

Following the Kite Realty Transaction, another REIT sold preferred stock with anti-Waldenization provisions, but taking an alternative approach. Cogdell Spencer, a small REIT specializing in the ownership of medical office buildings, issued a Series A preferred in December 2010 which features provisions protecting shareholders through conversion privileges. In the event of a 'fundamental change,' which is defined as a change of control and de-listing of the common stock, the preferred shareholder has the right to convert into common shares at the market price of the common stock (which is defined as the closing price on the average of the last 10 days). The formula is effectively that the number of common shares exchanged is the preferred liquidation price ($25) divided by the price of the common shares. The maximum number of common shares that may be given is 6.0125 per preferred share based on 70% of the Cogdell Spencer common stock price at the date of the preferred issuance. So if the Cogdell Spencer share price falls more than 30% below this level during the period of fundamental change, it is possible that a preferred shareholder could realize less than liquidation value.

Hudson Pacific

In contrast, in December 2010 Hudson Pacific Properties, a newly-formed West Coast Office REIT sold preferred stock ('Series B') without any anti-Waldenization provisions. This emphasizes the need to exercise caution, and take a quick review of the prospectus supplement (readily available through the SEC website 'EDGAR' or at 'Quantum on Line,' information sources which are discussed in the next chapter).

Protecting Yourself from Waldenization

So, there are encouraging signs that some new REIT Preferred issues are addressing the most serious risks faced by the investor. But what can the investor do to reduce the Waldenization in a portfolio of REIT Preferreds? There are no fail-safe solutions, but the risks of taking a below-the-water-line hit can be substantially reduced:

1. An increasing number of non-investment grade REIT Preferreds (from late 2010 forward) may contain the 4% privatization step-up in yield or the fundamental change conversion formula mentioned above. Look closely at REIT Preferreds issued in the fourth quarter of 2010 and later for issues with these provisions, as the shares are worth a premium, and will mitigate part of the risk. Note that investment grade REIT Preferreds will almost certainly not contain this provision.
2. Maintain portfolio diversity: I have 18 stocks in my REIT Preferred portfolio for the major reason of reducing the impact of Waldenization when it happens.
3. Weight your investments more heavily in larger companies, which are less likely to be taken private.
4. Be willing to invest in companies with complex structures that are unlikely to be taken private: one example of this is AIMCO, a large apartment REIT with a complex structure and a property portfolio of questionable market appeal, making it an unlikely acquisition candidate. But the company is financially sound, so highly likely to continue to pay its preferred dividends.
5. Investment grade companies are much less likely to be Waldenized: they are often committed to staying public, and thus tend to be less likely to be acquired.
6. Watch your portfolio and look for warning signs of an impending sale of the business. On the first rumor of a sale, or even after it has been announced, don't hesitate to sell your position, and move aggressively to liquidate your position ahead of anybody else.
7. Watch to see if the provisions covering the change of control and de-listing provisions featured in the Kite Realty Series A preferred or the Cogdell Spencer conversion structure become a standard for non-investment grade preferred. If so and if the pricing is favorable, seek opportunities to add Preferreds with one of these two provisions to your portfolio. To the extent you have Preferreds with these protections in your portfolio, you have reduced one of the biggest risks that you face, and you may consider reducing your diversification requirement.

One of the REITs in which I held a preferred position was to be Waldenized and I sold within a day of the announcement, and I broke even on my investment. In another case, I heard a rumor of a pending sale, and I sold my preferred stock position immediately (and took a short-term capital gain). The rumor proved to be false, but the risk of losses is so big that one cannot take these rumors lightly.

Credit Risk

We've seen that the Rating Agencies don't correctly assess the credit risks of REITs. Nonetheless, most of the REIT Preferreds that we'll choose to invest in are rated by the Rating Agencies as below investment grade, and so credit risk cannot be ignored. We have seen three REITs suspend their preferred dividends (of which one was reinstated after 7 missed quarters), and it seems probable that at least one more will renew payments.

As a group, REIT Preferreds have the strong advantage of being backed by hard assets that in most cases are fairly readily saleable. The liquidity of the assets depends on the asset class (Apartments tend to be the most liquid. Some more esoteric property types such as movie theatres or prisons may be the least marketable!). Everything else being equal, preferred shareholders of REITs should have a better chance of protecting their principal than preferred shareholders of non-REITs.

Mitigating your credit risk

There are some fairly straight forward ways of mitigating credit risk:

a) Maintain a broad diversity of preferred stocks in your portfolio. This includes not only investing in a broad basket of stocks, but also in a cross section of property types.
b) The more risk averse you are, increase your allocation to investment grade companies and investment grade stocks.
c) Look carefully at Preferreds that are trading at yields which are significantly above the averages for the sector, property type, and rating. These are the biggest opportunities, but they need to be investigated carefully. Review the basic financial statistics, and be sure to review the latest quarterly financial report, the investor conference call, and investor presentations (all found on the company's website).

One of my rules is that prior to making an investment in any preferred stock, regardless of the apparent strength of the Company, I always conduct the review mentioned in (c) above. I'm looking for signals about business and strategy trends that might affect the credit of the Company. Following an investment, monitor the quarterly reports of each Company regularly, and for any Company that is particularly risky, also monitor the conference call.

Improving credit

As you will see in the section on investment strategy, investing in Companies that are in transition is a great way for REIT Preferred shareholders to make money. Companies strengthening their balance sheets and businesses can result in gains to the preferred shareholder. However, this can also lead to an eventual 'call' of the preferred stock: once the Company has successfully repositioned its business and its balance sheet, it may be able to reduce its capital costs by replacing the current preferred stock with a new preferred issuance (at a lower dividend yield) or with a combination of common equity and debt. If the stock is called, you recover your principal in its entirety, and often make a nice capital profit if you have purchased the stock for less than its call price of $25, but you have to find an alternative preferred stock to invest in, hopefully to maintain the same level of return after paying tax on the gain.

There is a lesser chance that the improvement can also lead to a sale of the Company and the possible Waldenization, and thus increase risk to your principal, which emphasizes the need to be pro-active in managing risk.

Interest Rate: Consider your goals

For many investors in or approaching retirement, the major objective is to have a secure source of regular income. Those without a defined benefit pension plan might consider a version of the strategy described in this book, as it is possible to set up a reasonably assured income stream using REIT Preferred.

In this case, the investor may be less focused on the risk of principal erosion from interest rate movements, but more interested in preserving the income stream. A well-diversified portfolio with shares bought below the call price can achieve this under most normal circumstances. A reduction in value caused by an increase in interest rates will make it less likely that the underlying preferred stock will be called, further assuring the income stream.

In this case, the investor is focused only on long-term values, and ignores cyclical valuation changes due to movements in prevailing interest rates, and can narrow the investment focus to monitor changes in credit quality and risks of Waldenization.

While this income stream is not protected against inflation, remember that the allocation to REIT Preferred stocks should be a small part of an investor's investment portfolio, and that addressing inflation risks needs to be done through maintaining portfolio diversity and investing also in other asset types.

CHAPTER 13

Investment Strategy: Setting Up

You're solvent if you don't have to smooth down your hair and straighten your tie when you go into the bank for a loan.

With this background in mind we can develop the principals of an investment strategy:

Go-it-alone or pick a Mutual Fund

Unfortunately, there are no REIT Preferred ETFs, and because of the small size of the market and relative illiquidity of the REIT Preferreds, there are not likely to be any in the future.

There is one excellent REIT Preferred mutual fund, the Forward Select Income Fund, which mainly invests in REIT Preferred stock, but not exclusively. It owns 130 different securities, and although some of these are issued by the same company, the Fund is very broadly diversified. Fund management is experienced and well respected.

The Fund is managed by Joel Beam, is based in San Francisco, and has a solid (if volatile) track record, with an average annual total return of 10.5% to shareholders over the past nine years (through August 31, 2010):

Forward Select Income A				*Data through 8-21-10*					
	2010	2009	2008	2007	2006	2005	2004	2003	2002
Total Return	18.3%	75.0%	-40.4%	-24.2%	15.6%	-2.0%	11.3%	24.0%	16.9%
Assets ($MM)	583	442	208	248	484	445	535	474	212

Source: Morningstar

Chart 23

CASH IS KING

There are several reasons why the investor with the time, confidence, and some investment experience may find 'going it alone' more financially rewarding than investing in the Forward Select Income Fund:

1. The Fund has an annual expense load of approximately 1.5%, which although reasonable is significant against a total return after expenses of 10.5%
2. The strategy and objectives of the Fund are practical given the constraints within which it has to operate, but not necessarily those that I endorse:
   - It holds a very broad and extremely large cross-section of companies, including a heavy representation of securities from the more highly rated REITs.
   - The Fund uses leverage to attain its goals, which to some of us can be scary (it can exaggerate volatility).
   - As with all mutual funds, the tax goals of the Fund may not reflect those of the investors.

Nonetheless, the Fund is a viable option for many.

The start: assembling the investment tools

1. Select Your Sources of Data on REIT Preferreds

BMO REIT Preferred Weekly

You need a readily available source of information on REIT stocks. The one I have found to be most useful is published by the Bank of Montreal, the BMO REIT Preferred Weekly. This has a pretty complete list of REIT Preferreds listed by property type which is published by the excellent REIT analyst team at BMO (the fact that BMO is a Canadian bank doesn't matter: BMO maintains a strong analytical and banking presence in the USA), and the weekly report includes most of the information for each preferred that you will need to screen stocks. The good news is that this is available in Excel format, so it is easily adapted to a format that you may find most useful.

A source of summary investment and financial data on REITs

There are a number of investment banks that publish excellent summaries of the REIT category which contain such data as the REITs' Senior Debt Ratings as published by Moody's and Standard & Poor's. The one I use is published weekly by KeyBanc, and, like the BMO data, it is published in Excel, so it is easy to sort and print the data that you need. Most of this data is assembled from SNL Financial, a source of financial data for investors, and is generally accurate enough for our purposes. However it is sometimes out of date: for instance, a REIT may have a change of investment rating, and the summary data in this publication may not pick this up for a month or more.

Quantum On Line

This is a general website, www.quantumonline.com, devoted to investing in income securities, and is extremely well done. You can access data on every REIT Preferred security that is of interest.

Yahoo

My own preference is to access stock data on Yahoo, and I maintain data on my REIT Preferred on Yahoo, set up as a portfolio. You'll want to include at least the ticker, price, change, and volume on the screen.

You can also set up your Yahoo screen to keep up with your portfolio's performance, which is something that I have found helpful. This is pretty simple to do.

You will find that the ticker designations for REIT Preferreds seem to vary between brokerage houses and websites, but these are generally limited to a few alternatives. Some preferred stocks are designated with the suffix "+A" to designate the Series Preferred A, others will use "-PA", "_PA, or "PRA". The differences can be frustrating, but are easily worked through.

It is also helpful to set up a separate Yahoo screen for the Common Stock (not the preferred stock) of the companies that you are tracking. This will enable you to view news items that affect each company as it is picked up by Yahoo (company news is generally not picked up on the preferred screen).

Raymond James

The REIT research team at Raymond James is one of the best in the sector, and they publish the REIT Preferred Quarterly. The report has excellent background information on REIT Preferreds, as well as comments and information on a limited number of REIT Preferreds that

Raymond James analysts follow. They do not make recommendations on individual preferreds.

Public Issuing Company websites

All public REITs maintain websites with sections devoted to investors. You can review company press releases, quarterly financial statements, and SEC filings, and listen to conference calls for a period of time after the call (some maintain transcripts of the call).

SEC ('EDGAR')

The SEC maintains an excellent website called EDGAR with the filings of all public companies at ***http://www.sec.gov/edgar/ searchedgar/companysearch.html***

You can access 10-K annual report and copies of quarterly financial reports, although I have found the individual company websites to be adequate almost all of the time.

2. Set up a brokerage account

Select a broker you are comfortable with, possibly considering one that can provide you with some of the research discussed above. My own preference is to trade through an on-line account which maintains current trading information, including bid and ask pricing on each REIT Preferred.

You may wish to consider opening an account with Raymond James which has an active REIT Research team so that you can be assured of obtaining their research. Since Raymond James is active with new issues of REIT Preferreds, an account may also gain you the opportunity to purchase new series of preferred at a favorable net price.

3. Set up a portfolio tracking system

You will need a simple spreadsheet designed to:

1. Track purchases and sales.
2. Evaluate yield.
3. Track dividend amounts and dates that the shares go ex-dividend and that dividends are paid.
4. Track the stock's investment rating and the issuer's fixed charge coverage.

5. Evaluate the risk of the shares being called.
6. Manage the tax treatment for any capital gains or losses.

Using the information on the spreadsheet, you can evaluate the yield after taxes and then calculate whether it is advisable to do an early sale or to continue the hold the stock. This can be used to evaluate the relative pricing of the current portfolio, and have almost all the information you need to make buy/sell decisions when used in concert with the BMO Preferred Weekly.

You can download prices from the Yahoo screen to a spread sheet, and then copy and paste the prices to this sheet periodically to keep the file updated.

4. Set up a preferred screening sheet

I have found it helpful to establish a spread sheet that highlights stocks that I'm tracking for future investment. This includes the same key information as the sheet above, except it obviously excludes the purchase and sale information.

CHAPTER 14

When to Hold and When to Fold

*A Bull Market is a random market movement causing an
investor to mistake himself for a financial genius.*

*Three economists went out hunting, and came across a
large deer. The first economist fired, but missed, by a yard to
the left. The second economist fired, but also missed, by
a yard to the right. The third economist didn't fire, but
shouted in triumph, "We got it! We got it!"*

We've discussed in Chapter 11 that there are two principal factors
that impact the pricing of the market for preferred stocks: changes in
Treasury bond interest rates and preferred dividend credit spreads.
Pricing of individual stocks is affected by the credit of each issuer.

Investor Goals

Long-term investors interested in generating income can be less
concerned about changes in interest rates. As for all investments, they
need to be concerned about investing all of their allocation to REIT
Preferreds at the peak of the market, and thus should consider dollar-
cost averaging, and taking a period of time to build their investment
position is the smartest way to proceed. Once the position is built,
then most of their management time can be limited to monitoring the
portfolio and making adjustments for changes in credit quality.

'Dollar-Cost Average': For those investors who do not need the
current income and are still in a mode of building their investment/

retirement portfolio, it is a sound practice to modify this strategy to use the dividend income generated to continue to invest, and dollar-cost average. In this way, every few months you can selectively add new stocks, further spreading your risk, and take account of price and market changes at the same time as you are looking at making adjustments to your portfolio.

Treasury Bonds

For investors concerned about changes in value and protecting principal values, tracking projections of the interest rate for the 10-Year Treasury bond is important. If rates are expected to increase, it may be time to reduce exposure to preferred stock, just as projected lower rates may indicate the time to increase exposure. There are many good sources of this information, but keeping up with economic and monetary trends through the Economist, financial newspapers, or various economic websites may be the best solution. As an example, at the present time most expect the yield on 10-year Treasuries to rise. Although inflation indicators are at worst mild, monetary policies have run their course, and the growth in the economy is slowly building. As we've seen, the yield on the 10-year Treasury bond increased by 100 bps in the latter couple of months of 2010, and further modest increases seem likely.

Identifying signals in the economy that indicate changes in long-term interest rates is difficult and needs a certain amount of courage. Often the decision by the Fed to reduce short-term interest rates presages a rise in long-term interest rates, since inflationary pressures will ultimately start to build. Current actions by the Fed to attempt to bring down long-term interest rates through 'quantitative easing' should be successful unless it is seen as a forerunner of future inflation. Making some judgment about where we are in the business cycle can help in this. For instance, it is widely believed that while at present inflation is very low, Fed action to increase the money supply, and de facto devalue the dollar, coupled with the lack of fiscal discipline by the Federal Government will inevitably lead to inflation and rising long-term interest rates. Projections of the 10-year Treasury bond show it increasing by up to 1% (100 bps), and thus it is important to consider this in evaluating the allocation of dollars to preferred stock.

Thus we expect little change in REIT Preferred valuations, but after that we may be approaching a time when it may be prudent to slow down our additions to the preferred stock allocation.

Credit Spreads

We've seen that on average over the past 10 years, REIT Preferred yields have averaged approximately 375 bps over 10-year Treasuries. As we have discussed, using some simple processes we can identify a diverse portfolio of REIT Preferreds which can increase this spread to 450 bps over the 10-Year Treasury. If we also include companies with a credit profile that is likely to improve, we can also have upside pricing potential in the portfolio.

We make a strong argument that this level of return from a portfolio of REIT Preferreds is better on a risk-adjusted basis than for many other types of investments.

When average credit spreads are above this level we should feel good about growing our preferred stock allocation, and at levels below this have a level of concern.

As an example, assume the average REIT Preferred stock yields 7.3%, indicating an approximate credit spread of 3.8% (380 bps) above the 10-year Treasury Bond rate of 3.5% (up from 2.5% in mid-October 2010). Thus we have some comfort that the credit spread is reasonably in line with its long-run level, but we do need to be concerned that future increases may adversely impact REIT Preferred pricing.

In conclusion, we have some favorable signals that inflation is currently low, and spreads of REIT Preferred yields to the 10-year Treasury are normal, indicating that it is now a reasonable time to buy REIT Preferreds. On the other hand, 10-year Treasury yields are likely to rise further, and we need to be concerned that in the longer run, monetary policy will cause yields to rise, driving REIT Preferred yields higher. This indicates that it may be appropriate to build or maintain a moderate allocation to REIT Preferreds.

Using this type of logic to drive your investment allocations is certainly not fool-proof, but has a sound basis.

Investment Allocation

There is no magic formula about how much to invest in REIT Preferred. It certainly should not form the major part of an investor's portfolio due to the interest rate risk (the individual credit risk is adequately addressed through diversification). The stocks also trade with relatively low volume, so it is appropriate to limit exposure to 5%-15% of a typical investment portfolio (for all investors, maintaining a good cross-section of investments in different asset types is essential). The allocation needs to be sufficiently large to hold 10 – 20 individual stocks to mitigate risk.

No one stock should represent more than 15% of your REIT Preferred allocation, and a better percentage may be 10%. The Waldenization risk (when companies are taken private, but the preferred stock is left 'hanging' as a publicly traded stock of a highly leveraged private REIT) is real, emphasizing the need for diversity in the portfolio, but there are exceptions to this 10-15% limitation. As we've discussed, some of the non-investment grade REIT Preferreds issued since late 2010 may offer more protection against Waldenization, as may stocks issued by very large REITs and those with investment grade ratings: management of these companies have generally a significant investment in the future of the business, and, of course, it is harder for a potential acquirer to take out the larger companies.

Mortgage REITs are separate animals from regular property-owning REITs, and the financing options open to Mortgage REITs are more limited. As a result, preferred issues of Mortgage REITs tend to deliver higher yields. I limit my exposure to Mortgage REITS to no more than 5% of the total preferred allocation.

Finally, it is wise to pick from several asset types. Some businesses are inherently more risky than others. For instance, Lodging is more risky than Multifamily, and as attractive as the returns can be from Lodging REIT Preferreds, it is good to limit exposure to that category to a reasonable level.

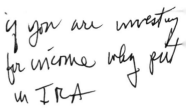
if you are investing for income why put in IRA

CHAPTER 15

Implementing Your Investment Strategy

Why has astrology been invented? So that stock market analysis could be an accurate science.

When possible, use your IRA

As we discussed, at the present time, the taxable portion of REIT dividends (including both common stock and preferred stock dividends) are taxable at an individual's personal tax rate. So, in the current tax environment where long-term capital gains rates are less than half ordinary income rates, owning REIT Preferreds in a tax-advantaged account such as an IRA makes a lot of sense. It makes more sense to concentrate investments such as non-REIT common and even non-REIT Preferred stocks in taxable accounts to take advantage of the lower tax rates for the dividends of these stocks, while keeping most of your REIT investments, and especially REIT Preferreds, in the tax-advantaged accounts.

Stock-picking

There are 152 REIT Perpetual Preferred series outstanding by 64 REITs. Your objective is to locate at least 10 different REITs from this universe with preferred series that have:

a. Attractive current yields
b. Upside price opportunity and
c. Price matched to credit risk

Selecting companies with the right balance of yield and risk

Many investors in REIT Preferreds are focused on credit risk, instead of the much more potent risks that we discussed earlier. The risks are predominately Waldenization (taking the REIT private, but leaving the preferred outstanding) and interest rates. A rise in long-term interest rates can devastate prices.

My proposed strategy intends to take advantage of the mispricing of risk of the entire REIT Preferred sector, both because the category is relatively small and somewhat overlooked by the professional and institutional investor class, and because the rating agencies are overly conservative and in many cases don't rate REITs and REIT Preferreds highly enough. The mispricing opportunity is for both investment grade and non-investment grade securities, but is particularly concentrated in the non-investment grade category.

Most investors favor higher grade REIT Preferreds, and especially those with an investment grade (Baa3/BBB+ or above). Income investors tend to be heavily focused on the stock ratings of the rating agencies for two major reasons: the rating agencies do the investment and due diligence analysis on behalf of the investor, thereby providing an authoritative third-party endorsement of the investment, and the rating 'investment grade' is a seal of approval that institutional and retail investors find comforting (some institutional investors are required to limit their investments to investment grade securities). As a result, pricing of the high grade Preferreds of the 14 companies that have issued investment grade Preferreds is generally too high relative to pricing on non-investment grade Preferreds. The yield on this high grade Preferreds averages 6.9% (at the time of writing), 1.2% less than for the 31 non-investment grade REITs that have issued non-investment grade and non-rated Preferreds.

REITS with Investment Grade Perpetual Preferred				
		Rating		
Category	REIT	Moody's	S & P	Comment
Apartment	BRE	Baa3	BB+	Split-rated (S&P below Investment Grade)
Apartment	EQR	Baa2	BBB-	
Apartment	UDR	Baa3	BB+	Split-rated (S&P below Investment Grade)
Self-Storage	PSA	Baa1	BBB	
Office	CHW	Baa3	BB+	Split-rated (S&P below Investment Grade)
Industrial	AMB	Baa2	BB+	Split-rated (S&P below Investment Grade)
Industrial	PLD	Baa3	BB	Split-rated (S&P below Investment Grade)
Mall	SPG	Baa1	BBB	
Shopping Center	KIM		BBB-	
Shopping Center	SKT	Baa3	BB+	Split-rated (S&P below Investment Grade)
Shopping Center	WRI	Baa3	BB+	Split-rated (S&P below Investment Grade)
Retail	O	Baa2	BB+	Split-rated (S&P below Investment Grade)
Healthcare	HCN	Baa3	BB	Split-rated (S&P below Investment Grade)
Diversified	VNO	Baa3		

Chart 24

Similarly, the pricing of the Preferreds issued by the 13 companies with an investment grade senior debt rating, but a preferred rating that is below-investment grade, is also sometimes out of reach. However, there are likely to be some potential opportunities in this category:

• Some investors will limit their exposure to investment grade Preferreds (despite the senior debt of the company being rated investment grade). In other words, some investors buy into the severe downgrading of REIT Preferreds by the rating agencies.

- Some less sophisticated investors may not appreciate that there is an investment grade company backing the preferred. The simple screening tools may not highlight this. And remember that the REIT Preferred category is overlooked by most sophisticated institutional investors.

At the present time, the yield on these Preferreds is 7.4%, 0.7% below the yield of the 29 non-investment grade REIT issuers.

Investment Grade REITS with non-Investment Grade Perpetual Preferred			
		Senior Debt Rating	
Category	REIT	Moody's	S & P
Apartment	PPS		BBB-
Office	BMR	Baa3	BBB-
	BDN		BBB-
	DLR	Baa2	BBB-
	DRE		BBB-
	HIW		BBB-
	KRC		BBB-
	PSB		BBB
Shopping Center	REG		BBB
Diversified	NNN		BBB-
Lodging	HPT		BBB-
Healthcare	HCP	BBB	
Specialty	EPR	Baa2	

Chart 25

There are 31 REITs that are rated below investment grade or are otherwise not rated that have issued Preferreds. The best risk/reward is generally found within this group. At the time of writing the average yield for this group is 8.1%.

REITS below Investment Grade or Unrated, with Preferred outstanding*			
		Senior Debt Rating	
Category	REIT	Moody's	S & P
Apartment	AIV		BB+
Office	ARE		
	OFC		
	MPG		
	PKY		
	SLG		BB+
	DFT		BB-
Industrial	FR		B+
	MNR		
Malls	CBL		
	GRT		B+
	TCO		
Shopping Center	CDR		
	DDR		BB
	BFS		
	KRG		
	UBP		
Healthcare	LTC		
	CSA		
	OHI		BB
Diversified	CUZ		
	LSE		
	LXP		
	PGP		
Lodging	AHT		
	FCH		B-
	HT		
	LHO		
	BEE		
	SHO		
	SPPRP		

*Excludes mortgage REITs and convertible preferred

Chart 26

In addition, there are 11 mortgage REITs with preferred stock, all of which are unrated or below investment grade. Mortgage REITs have more limited access to capital, as it is difficult for them to provide a good security interest in liquid collateral, so they necessarily have to tap the unsecured debt or bank credit markets. You may wish to research some of these REITs with a view to making what may be a more speculative investment, with one of the reasons being their high yield (an average of 9.3%). My own preferred stock portfolio has just a 5% allocation to a single Mortgage REIT, which I regard as somewhat speculative, but which has been selected with limited underwriting, and using some of the same criteria that I use for non-Mortgage REITs. The amount of research that I have performed on Mortgage REITs is extremely limited, and it is not a category that I have so far become comfortable with.

Mortgage REITS with Preferred
ANH
CMO
GOOD
IMP
MFA
NCT
NLY
NOVSP
NRF
RAS
SFI

Chart 27

Stock Selection

You've now separated your main universe of preferred stocks into three categories (excluding Mortgage REITs):

1. Investment Grade/Split Rated Preferred
2. Companies with Investment Grade Senior Debt Ratings, and non-Investment Grade Preferreds
3. Below-Investment Grade and Non-Rated Companies

A combination of the following will highlight stocks for more detailed analysis:

Step 1: Look for Preferreds with above average yield by category of Credit Rating.

Look for stocks within each of these categories which offer yields above the category average. For instance we know that the average yield for Category 2 is 7.4%, yet there are preferred series yielding from as low as 6.8% to a high of 8.5%. So, start with the highest yielding outliers and work down the list.

Step 2: Don't pay more than $25.50 per share, and generally have a price limit of $25.

Most of the perpetual preferred stocks are currently callable, usually at $25, with a few outliers, which makes them ineligible for calling until the five years is up). Rather than getting involved in yield-to-call calculations, I try to pick stocks that are priced at no more than $25 plus one quarter's dividend (or around $25.50 per share). This means that I won't lose very much if the stock is called.

More sophisticated investors may wish to consider using the yield-to-call calculations, but since there are relatively few REIT Preferreds that are not currently callable, this may be more brain damage than you want to incur. Stick with the guideline of a price limitation of $25.50.

You will find a few stocks without call prices, or a call price other than $25, or other odd features: most of these are convertible preferred that I recommend avoiding (too complicated to bother with), or have some other features that may present opportunity, but may also contain traps for the unwary.

Remember that $25 plus one month's dividend is the absolute maximum price: generally you should select stocks that are below the call price, $25, because then there is potential for the price to move up to the call price, and you have the opportunity for a capital gain. You also have less risk that the stock will be called.

If the stock is trading much below its call price, it indicates one or both of the following:

- interest rates have risen since the original issuance date, causing the price to drop
- the issuer's credit rating or perceived financial strength has dropped since the original issuance date.

In either case, there is potential for pricing upside, and you can perform further research (check the issuer's quarterly report and conference call) to assess the likelihood of positive price movement.

Those stocks with the biggest gap between current price and call price have the most upside potential. This is very important, as it not only represents upside opportunity, but also represents downside protection. Owning stock that you expect to have an improved credit profile leading to higher pricing is the best protection against pricing risk due to a rise in interest rates.

If the stock is trading steadily at or around its maximum ($25 plus one month's dividend) and the yield is well above the average for the pricing group, beware of a likely 'call' of the stock sooner rather than later. For instance, if the stock is trading at 7.5% at $25.50 per share, and the average yield for stocks in the investment grade group is 6.9%, there is a very good chance that the stock will be called by the issuing REIT. So, if you've paid a premium above the call price, you will lose the premium. But if you've paid $25 or less, you will enjoy a nice risk-adjusted return until the stock is called; and the chances are if you pay between $25 and $25.50, you will still enjoy a nice return, since it is unlikely that the stock will be called immediately, and there is always a chance that the preferred will not be called.

On your spread sheet you need to be looking closely at the date the stock goes ex-dividend, because clearly if the quarterly dividend is 50 cents, you should expect a quarterly price swing of this amount, and you need to take this (in other words, the 'Strip Yield' discussed in Chapter 8) into account in the price you are willing to pay. A spread sheet incorporating the Strip Yield of the stocks you are tracking is not hard to maintain, although my own approach (as a long-term holder) is to do this analysis informally. The actual dividend impact will depend if you're investing in a tax-free account such as an IRA or in a taxable account; obviously in the latter case, you're less interested in capturing the dividend and more interested in capturing price appreciation. The market for REIT Preferreds is far from perfect, and there are price aberrations from time to time which you can position yourself to take advantage of.

Step 3: Compare the price to credit risk.

Once you've identified some companies with a preferred series whose yield is apparently higher than its credit group peers, it is time to do a little more research. This is easily done initially through a review of the fixed charge coverage of the company as reported in the BMO REIT Preferred Weekly, comparing the company to its sector average.

More interesting and perhaps more relevant is a review of credit trends of the individual companies. This is achieved through a brief review of the results and management comments in the companies' quarterly press releases. Listening to the conference call or reading the call transcripts is also helpful. You are simply looking for comments concerning credit trends. For instance, one company has made it public that management's bonuses are tied to improvement in its balance sheet. Others make public statements about improving balance sheet strength. One weak company received an equity capital infusion from a large foreign investor, and since the investor is very unlikely to walk away from its investment, it seems obvious that the company's balance sheet and financial position is likely to improve. Some of this may be dilutive to common stock holders, but very beneficial to preferred shareholders.

Those investors with sturdy constitutions can allocate a limited part of their investment funds to some of the more speculative preferred stocks, where the likelihood of the company missing (or deferring) a preferred dividend seems higher. Again it is important to weigh the probability that the company will manage to improve its balance sheet sufficiently by raising common equity or selling assets while avoiding selling out completely (raising the Waldenization specter).

In most cases of weak credit, public company management will preserve their jobs and preserve their independence by shoring up the balance sheet when necessary through the issuance of common stock or the sale of assets. It is reasonable to expect (but not guaranteed) that REITs with leveraged balance sheets will eventually have the opportunity to address the problem through one of these two methods, to the ultimate benefit of the preferred stockholders. Most REITs have sound assets and access to the capital markets most of the time that provides them with time and alternatives to address their balance sheet problems. A cursory review of quarterly and annual reports will tell you relatively quickly those that are unacceptably risky (often those facing large development pipelines with large risky projects).

Step 4. Select stocks with Change of Control Protection.

It is worthwhile conducting an early screening for REIT Preferred issues which contain some change of control protection, especially the 4% dividend step-up provision upon the privatization of the REIT (Kite Realty provision) or the 'fundamental change' conversion right (Cogdell Spencer provision). These are new developments at the time of writing, but are likely to apply to non-investment grade preferred series issued in the last quarter of 2010 and later. Check the prospectus for this provision (Quantum on Line is a good source of prospectuses of preferreds, but they are also available on the SEC website, EDGAR). These stocks are worth a premium.

Step 5. Select the preferred series.

Forty-one REITs have more than one series of preferred outstanding. One REIT, Public Storage, has outstanding no less than 17 different series, while 21 REITs have only one series outstanding. So, once you have selected the REIT that you like, in the majority of cases, you need to pick the Series to invest in. The rating on each perpetual preferred series of any one company is almost always the same, and all the series carry identical credit risks. Thus you are looking for differences in yield as the primary decision driver, but there are subtle differences you'll also want to consider.

While you are interested primarily in the series with the highest yield (assuming everything else is equal), as a secondary consideration favor the series that are trading at the lowest absolute price. This series will have the best opportunity for favorable price movement should the company's credit improve (positive changes in credit are your biggest opportunity). The series with the lowest absolute price will also obviously tend to be the last series to be called in the event all the company's preferred series improve in price.

Another consideration is the liquidity of the series. You will find that for the same company, average daily trading volume varies by preferred series. Most often, the larger the number of outstanding shares, the more it trades. Generally, it is safest to favor the larger, higher volume series, as these are the most liquid, and this is beneficial when it is time to sell.

The issue date (and thus the initial call date, typically five years from the date of issue) is also a consideration. The further away the call date, the more time you are assured of being able to hold the stock.

As mentioned above, there may be a recent series with the 4% go-private dividend step-up, and these are worth seeking as they are worth a small premium.

After these considerations and you have narrowed down your focus to one or two series, then you will find it makes sense to watch each series for an entry point, taking into account the ex-dividend date of each.

Step 6. Implementation: Buy stock.
You should now be ready to target individual shares that interest you, and have established price parameters. You can start to review their trading performance over a period of time.

When you get ready to place your buy orders, complete your Excel spread sheet with all the necessary information, such as outlined in the Appendix, including the key dividend dates so that you can correctly price the stock.

The relatively thin trading of most REIT Preferred stock necessitates that you place a tight limit on the price around which you're a buyer. Establishing a position in a stock can involve some work, and patience is important, as is not hitting the market all at one time with large orders.

Dollar-Cost Average: Take time to invest, and absent other information, spread your investments over a period of time to avoid market spikes. If you don't need the current income, consider investing the dividend income to diversify your portfolio and to spread your investment timing risk.

Step 7: Evaluate your portfolio.

Evaluating your portfolio once a quarter is a good discipline, and it is generally convenient to use this once the companies have reported their results. This is a good time to match total REIT Preferred yields against the 10-year Treasury yield, and check changes in current yield, credit quality and additions to the REIT Preferred universe, reinvest dividends (if appropriate), and implement appropriate changes.

CHAPTER 16

Some Examples

The following are some examples from my own experience of investing in REIT Preferreds.. They represent some different types of opportunities to garner what I believe to be excess yield or excess opportunity for capital appreciation. Generally, if you can acquire stocks yielding more than they 'ought' to be yielding, this will lead to capital appreciation when the market realizes the disparity. There are some cases where the market never does wake up to the disparity (good news if you want to keep investing), and as we have noted, this tends to be the case for the large majority of REIT Preferreds as they are rated below investment grade.

Ashford Hospitality Trust Preferred Series D

I started to purchase this stock in September 2010, but mainly established the position in October, with a final addition in December 2010. My average cost is $22.83 per share (including commissions), and the stock is now priced at $23.35, after going ex-dividend (the stock pays a quarterly dividend of $0.50281).

The stock is not callable until July 2012; this is not a concern at present as the stock is trading well under the $25 call price.

I became interested in Ashford's preferred stock when I spotted that Ashford was going to sell some additional Preferred stock (they sold $75MM). They had two series outstanding, Series A and Series D, and they planned to add to the Series D. I selected the Series 'D' (as opposed to the Series 'A') for three reasons:

- It is more liquid: ($200 million outstanding for the Series D compared to $35 million for the Series A).

- Unlike the Series A, the Series D is not currently callable.
- Despite identical dividend dates, pricing was more attractive on the Series D, probably due to market disruptions from the additional offering (see below).

Ashford is a fairly large REIT for a hotel REIT, ($3.5 billion total enterprise value) and seems to be well entrenched with professional management. It is suffering from too much debt and too little equity (57% debt/gross assets, compared to a sector average of 49%). I reviewed their press releases and most recent conference call, and could see that they were making a serious effort to shore-up their balance sheet and address debt maturities which were the biggest concerns of investors, and, in fact, the additional sale of the Series D allowed them to pay down their credit line. Their press release also indicated that they may use some of the proceeds of the Preferred sale to repurchase a convertible preferred, which was encouraging: it meant that they were interested in playing offense, in other words, not just consumed with worries of debt maturities.

Ashford is not rated by either of the two major rating agencies. Its fixed charge coverage is over 2, not great, but certainly not in the critical care ward. It has suspended dividend payments on its common shares, which is certainly not a sign of strength, but this is not necessarily a critical issue for preferred shareholders.

My first purchase of the stock was the day after the offering closed; often, after a stock offering, the shares will trade down, and so I spotted that the Preferred Series D sold down to $22.90 a share from the offering price of $23.18. The stock was about to go ex-dividend, and so I considered the fact that I was getting the 50-cent dividend (30-cents after tax) 'free.' The initial yield of 9.2% rises to 9.35% after considering the imminent payment of the 'free' 30-cent dividend (net of tax).

The initial yield of 9.35% compared to a weighted average of 7.7% for the lodging sector as a whole, and this seemed to represent an attractive buy based on my perception of the risk of the investment. Key to the decision was the likelihood that Ashford's financial position was set to strengthen as a result of management actions, and that the outlook both for revenues and asset valuations in the lodging industry was rapidly improving. I added to the position as cash became available in October, and then on December 15 Ashford announced a $70 million common stock sale had closed that day. I immediately purchased additional Preferred D shares (at $22.97 a share), betting that the Preferred share pricing would soon reflect the stronger balance sheet (which turned out to be the case, although the positive market reaction has not been as strong as I expected). With the Preferred now yielding 9.0% immediately ex-dividend, I believe there is still upside remaining on a relatively solid company with an improving outlook.

Developers Diversified Realty Preferred Series I

I was attracted to this stock initially in June 2009 because of the spectacular yield (16.4%). Although the REIT Preferred market at that time was floundering, the yield on this stock indicated that investors believed that the Company was in serious trouble.

Developers Diversified is a large shopping center company with international investments, and it was in serious trouble. Debt maturities, collapsed value of its shopping center assets, floundering developments, and an overstretched balance sheet compounded with the market financial crisis to place it in a serious position. It seemed that it was writing down investment values continuously. Despite all of this, I was encouraged that its Preferred stock was rated Ba1 by Moody's and B by S&P, which is far from investment grade, but not terrible considering the situation.

The key to the investment decision was that a sophisticated investor, the (German) Otto family, had just made a $110 million equity investment and obtained additional warrants to invest more. Reviewing the Company's public filings with the SEC, the conference calls, and its investor presentations (all available on its website) made it evident that the Company was actively refinancing debt, selling assets, and working hard on a plan to generate liquidity.

Once I became aware of the Otto family investment and completed the research above, in mid-June 2009 I made (for me) a relatively large investment in the Series I Preferred, choosing this series over two others because of a marginally higher yield.

In this case the call date was not a factor in picking which of three preferred series that Developers Diversified had outstanding. Price was a factor: the Series G was trading at around $12/share, compared to $11.41 for the Series I, and although yields were comparable, the amount of price upside for the Series G was thus lower than for the Series I. My average price paid for the Series I was $11.41 per share (including commissions), and the stock is trading today (having just gone ex-dividend) for $23.75. I spaced the purchases out over a week in order to avoid stirring the market (all the Preferreds are thinly traded).

With the Preferred Series I now yielding only 7.9%, it is now fairly priced, and is one I would normally consider selling, but there still may be some pricing upside (the stock is trading 5% below its $25 call price) as the Company continues to dig itself out of its balance sheet and development issues. On a risk adjusted basis, it is also hard to replace the 7.9% yield after taking into consideration the tax owed on the gain.

Apartment Investment and Management Company (AIMCO) Preferred Series U

AIMCO is one of the largest apartment owners and operators with a total enterprise value of $10 billion. However they are one of the more highly leveraged of the apartment REITs, with 54% debt/gross assets, and 61% debt + preferred/gross assets. They also have substantial issues with their portfolio and complex corporate structure.

In 2009, the operating environment for all real estate companies was difficult, and AIMCO struggled more than most. It elected to drastically reduce its cash dividend on its common shares, and became heavily focused on repositioning its portfolio and balance sheet. Many investment analysts who followed the company believed that their efforts would be successful.

My decision to invest in August 2009 was based on AIMCO's repositioning efforts and my belief that AIMCO was not in such dire straits that it would fail. It was also too big (for the current state of the financial markets), and sufficiently complex that it would be unlikely to be taken private or otherwise purchased. It had access to attractive debt through Fannie Mae and Freddie Mac.

AIMCO's Preferreds are rated Ba3 and B+, well below investment grade, and the company's fixed charge coverage is only in the 1.6 range. However the company is reasonably stable, has no development to speak of, has good access to the capital markets, and demand for apartment housing is strong. Apartment asset pricing has also risen quite sharply.

In August 2009, I took a position in their Series U Preferred. There were five series of Preferred to choose from. As with DDR above, I picked the Series U because it had the most upside potential: it was originally priced when it was sold in 2004 to yield 7 3/8% (at $25 per share), compared to 8%, 7 7/8%, and 9 3/8% for the other four series. So, it is reasonable to think that the 7 3/8% Series U Preferred will take longer to return to $25, and have more upside potential.

My purchases in August were priced at $18.30 - $18.50 per share, yielding 10.5%. Based on the continued good progress of the company (according to investment analysts and company reports) and the strength of the apartment market, I added to the position in January and May 2010 at $22.17 and $22.90 per share. The 8.5% yield seemed to be attractive relative to other REIT Preferreds at the time, given the Company size and the balance sheet improvement it was committed to. At the end of 2010, the stock was priced at $25.15 per share after having just gone ex-dividend and yields 7.7%. This has now become a stock that seems to be a little pricey compared to all other REIT Preferreds, although not in comparison with those in the apartment sector which tends to trade at a slight premium, due to lower perceived sector risks. The tax gain makes the stock hard to replace at an attractive enough yield on a risk-adjusted basis.

BioMed Realty (BMR) Trust Preferred Series A

BioMed operates in a very narrow part of the real estate market providing research and lab space for the medical companies. Since the market is so specialized, the liquidity of their property types is limited, and so debt financing is not always easy to obtain except on a low leverage basis. In 2009 the company was performing well, and at the end of November released its third quarter results, and increased its earnings guidance. Although, as the Series A Preferred was priced at $21.00 and yielding a relatively modest (for then) 8.8%, it seemed a good conservative play.

In April the following year BMR announced that it had received an investment grade rating from Moody's and S&P, and sold unsecured notes. The company had also sold a lot of common stock in order to satisfy the rating agencies' capital requirements, so overall the company's balance sheet and credit profile had improved dramatically. So this is the perfect scenario for a preferred stock investor, where the value of the preferred stock has increased significantly through the company's actions. For various reasons I had been asleep at the switch, missed this announcement, and it was not until June that I picked up on this. Probably due to the lack of visibility within the REIT Preferred market the price of the Series A was still about $22.50, where it had been in January, yielding 8.2%, which was a high yield for an investment grade company at the time. So I added to the position, and by the end of 2010 the market had adjusted, and the stock was trading at $25 ex-dividend, and yielding 7.4%.

Although BMR is a high quality company and now investment grade, the upside has now most likely gone from the Series A, and the yield is relatively low even after paying capital gains tax, so it is likely that I will try to replace part of this holding with a higher yielding stock with more upside.

Conclusion

The examples above show how an initial screening for REIT Preferreds that are trading outside of the normal range for their category of company, followed by some simple research of material easily accessible on issuers' websites, can provide what you need to make a reasonably well-informed decision. The goal is to locate preferred issues that are under-priced currently and/or have upside based on an improvement in their financial position and market conditions (and by definition, trading below the call price of $25).

Sometimes building a position in a stock can be frustrating, and so patience may be needed, and on occasion it is necessary to wait for a period or select an alternative stock.

In planning your strategy, take these steps:

- Screen for stocks with dividend yields that are unjustifiably high.
- Look for companies that are committed to improving their balance sheets.
- Perform basic and straightforward desk-top research using companies' websites to understand the reasons for a stock's high yield or potential for appreciation.
- Buy stocks at less than $25 (or at most, $25 plus one quarter's dividend).
- Work within your price parameters for each stock.

CHAPTER 17

Summary and Conclusions

Real Estate Investment Trusts have proven to be an established and successful class of public companies that have performed well for investors. REIT Preferreds have also now matured into sound investments provided that reasonable caution is exercised. The initial possibility for spectacular investment returns has passed, but solid cash dividend yields in the 8% range should be readily achievable.

Active investors seeking dividend income can follow these basic guidelines to develop their investment programs

1. Manage Credit Risk

The biggest risks can be contained through diversification: be sure to have Preferreds from at least 10 REITs in your portfolio. For this reason, you will need to invest a minimum of just $10,000 - $20,000.

Look for REIT Preferreds newly issued in the latter part of 2010 and later that contain protections against going private (Waldenization).

2. Perform an initial screening

Using summary reports identify companies with out-size dividend yields. Focus especially on companies that are not investment grade, but as in the example of BMR in the previous chapter, every so often you can identify investment grade companies whose Preferreds are mispriced.

3. Due diligence

Perform the necessary due diligence on the companies identified in the initial screening: review the company's quarterly reports, investor presentations, and conference calls. Look for companies whose credit is improving or will improve (based on management actions and statements or market movements). Don't be afraid of large companies which may have less attractive balance sheets, but because of their size are unlikely to be acquired, provided the management seems to be competent.

4. Set the price parameters

Once you have identified the companies whose Preferreds you'd like to buy, if there is more than one Preferred series to choose from, select the series with the best combination of yield, call date, and liquidity. Consider the ex-dividend date, as this can make a significant difference to the yield, and often the dividends create market inefficiencies that can help you obtain a better price. Set the price that you are willing to pay, and then start watching the bid-ask activity preparatory to pulling the trigger to purchase the stock (with an established limit).

5. Manage interest rate risk

An increase in the risk-free interest rate – long-term Treasuries – can ultimately be expected to impact the price of REIT Preferreds negatively. Conversely, falling 10-year Treasury yields can ultimately be expected to help REIT Preferred prices to rise. Since none of us are smart enough to predict interest rates within any degree of precision (although we often think we can), it is important to maintain diversity in your investment portfolio, with REIT Preferreds and other investments which may be sensitive to changes in long-term interest rates as only a portion of your total investment portfolio. Few can be successful market timers over the long run.

Also, recognize that the objective for many investors will be to establish a REIT Preferred portfolio to provide long-term dividend income as part of a retirement portfolio, where relatively short-term fluctuations of value will not be so important.

The long-term average yield of REIT Preferreds has been 3.75% over the 10-year Treasury bond. With the current 10-year Treasury yielding just under 3.5%, and REIT Preferreds yielding 7.3% on average, we have about reached the 'right' pricing level for REIT

Preferreds. A significant further rise in Treasury yields may impact REIT Preferred prices, although it seems likely that prices will not be much impacted by a rise in Treasury yields perhaps to 4% or 4.5%, as credit spreads will likely contract with the expansion of the economy. Exercise caution in a rising interest rate environment, especially after the 10-year Treasury yield reaches beyond 4% - 4.5% until 10-year Treasury yields begin to peak. A good way to manage this risk is to invest cautiously over an extended period of one year or more.

Glossary

Adjusted Funds from Operations (AFFO): This is FFO, as defined below, less an allowance for capital reserves, often described as 'Recurring Capital Expenditures.' The intent of AFFO is that it should provide investors with a measure of performance after taking into account the capital expenditures needed to maintain the assets. Occasionally, institutional investors and analysts will exclude one-time charges from AFFO to attempt to normalize this measure.

Below investment grade: Securities that are rated below the four highest rating categories by one of the nationally recognized credit rating agencies, typically Moody's, Standard & Poor's, or Fitch's. In the case of Moody's this rating is Ba1 or below, or in the case of Fitch or Standard & Poor's BB+ or below. Implied is the belief of the rating agencies that the securities are in their judgment inherently risky. Many investors choose to avoid these securities, and some institutions avoid them by policy. Since the financial debacle of late 2008 and 2009 many mortgage bonds that were very highly rated by the credit rating agencies were proven to be catastrophically over-rated. It has generally been accepted that investors need to perform their own credit assessment of securities, but time constraints make this impractical for most investors. The author contends that the rating agencies under-rate REIT Preferred securities.

Black Swan event: Refers to an event which is generally regarded as being unpredictable. One of the most famous was the calamitous confluence of events that triggered the collapse of Long Term Capital Management (LTCM) in 1998, which two Nobel Laureate economists employed by LTCM failed to anticipate.

BMO REIT Preferred Weekly: A weekly summary containing key investment data for almost all North American REIT Preferreds, published by the Bank of Montreal.

Call, Callable: In the context here, "call" refers to the ability of issuers of Preferred Shares to cash out the investor at a pre-set price. Usually this provision is within a five year period of the issuance date of the Preferred series, and subsequently the ability to call the preferred lapses. This 'free call' option held by the issuer has a significant value, and is a major disadvantage to the investor.

Call Price: The pre-set price at which a preferred security will be redeemed if it should be called. This is most often $25.00 per share.

Change of Control Protection: Preferred securities with change of control protection have in their prospectuses filed with the SEC special provisions that apply in the event the issuer is sold. The particular protection is against acquirers leaving the preferred securities of an acquired company outstanding post-acquisition. There are some instances of limited protection being provided for preferred securities issued prior to the fall of 2010, generally an inadequate 1% increase in the dividend yield. The most effective provisions to protect investors came with some preferred series issued after this period. These provisions include a major step-up in dividend yield (4%) or the ability to convert the preferred to common shares according to a preset formula. In both of these instances, there is a reasonable chance that the Preferred shares would be redeemed in the event of an acquisition of the issuer, thus reducing one of the biggest risks of investing in REIT Preferreds.

Common Stock: The corporate equity of the company owned by the common shareholders, who elect the directors and vote on major corporate events in proportion to their ownership of common stock. The value of common stock rises and falls based on the demand for the stock, which is generally driven over the long run by the performance and financial strength of the company. Common stockholders are the most at risk in the event of bankruptcy.

Convertible Preferreds: Convertible Preferreds are convertible into common stock of the company at a fixed conversion ratio of a specified number of shares of common stock for each share of preferred stock. The conversion ratio can also be specified as a fixed price per common share in comparison to the liquidation preference value of the preferred shares. The conversion can generally take place any time at the holder's option. The company generally has the right to force conversion of the preferred shares into common shares when the market price of the common shares exceeds the conversion price by a specified amount. The initial conversion ratio is adjusted to account for stock splits, stock dividends, etc.

Cumulative: When a preferred dividend is cumulative, if the payment of any dividend is omitted, the omitted or unpaid dividend(s) is accrued and must be paid to the preferred holders before any dividends may be paid on the company's common stock. The accrued cumulative dividends also must be paid prior to or at the maturity date of the preferred or at the time the preferred is called.

Corporate Bonds: Corporate Bonds are a form of debt issued by corporations, often classified as investment grade by the rating agencies. Bonds generally have terms of more than one year, and sometimes have call features similar to preferred stock. Corporate Bonds pay interest at a pre-determined rate or a formula tied to a third-party index.

Credit Spreads: The premiums demanded by investors to buy non-Treasury securities. Put another way, the difference between the U.S. Treasury rate and an issuers' cost of debt, for debt of similar duration and terms.

Current Yield: The current yield for preferred stocks is calculated by comparing the fixed annual dividend or interest payment of a security to the current market price of the security and is expressed as a percentage of the current market price.

Debt: Debt represents an obligation of the issuer to pay fixed sums of money (principal plus interest) over a pre-defined term and in accordance with a credit or loan agreement. Missing a payment, or violating the terms of the credit agreement, can have significant negative consequences to the issuer. Debt owners usually have priority in payment before preferred and common shareholders.

Derivatives: These are financial instruments that can be purchased or sold which are linked to the value of an underlying asset. They have no intrinsic value of their own; they are dependant on the value of the underlying asset and future expected price changes. Typically derivatives are swaps, futures and options. They are a key ingredient in "hedging" an investment position.

Distribution: The distribution for preferred stock is the periodic payment of dividends, normally on a quarterly basis but occasionally on a monthly or other basis.

Dividends: Distributions made periodically by companies to shareholders of both common and preferred shares. Dividends are voted on periodically by the companies' boards of directors. Dividends to Preferred shareholders are a fixed amount and frequently made quarterly; missing a dividend payment can bring certain penalties to the company, but is not generally 'life threatening' such as is the case for missing an interest payment.

Dollar cost average: The practice of investing money over a period of time. As an example, if an investor has $12,000 to invest, he or she may invest $1,000 each month for a year, effectively purchasing the security at the average price for the year.

EDGAR: See Securities and Exchange Commission (SEC): the on-line data base of the SEC.

Exchange Traded Fund (ETF): ETFs are traded on the stock exchanges with a quoted price reflecting the price of their underlying investments. They can be actively traded by investors, just like individual stocks. Generally they carry lower fees than mutual funds, and while the most well-known ETFs track broad stock indices, in the last few years many actively managed ETFs have been established focusing on any sector of the market or investment style as described in the ETFs prospectus. ETFs 'borrow' their shares from investors, and concerns have been expressed periodically about their viability and safety. However, they seem to have become very well accepted, and almost everybody believes that they are here to stay.

Ex-dividend: The ex-dividend date for stocks is normally set two business days before the record date. If you purchase a stock on its ex-dividend date or after, you will not receive the next dividend payment. Instead, the seller gets the dividend. If you purchase before the ex-dividend date, you get the dividend.

Expense load: The fee that mutual funds charge investors to manage their funds. Most fees are deducted from investors' principal monthly or quarterly, but some funds also charge an initial or ending sales expense load. Many institutions also have what is known as 10b 5-1 expense loads, which are hidden costs of operating the fund wrapped into trading costs and other expenses of the fund.

Funds from Operations (FFO): This is the primary measure of performance for many REIT investors. It is generally defined as net income plus real estate depreciation, excluding any gains from asset sales. In other words it is a measure of the amount of cash that is generated from a REIT's assets each year, before any required capital expenditures. However, just like net income, FFO is not necessarily a pure performance measure, and you have to look at the composition of the numbers to understand the full picture.

Most companies define FFO in the manner prescribed by NAREIT, but not all do (especially small REITs).

Unlike net income, FFO is not a measure included within Generally Accepted Accounting Principles. Thus the Securities and Exchange Commission (SEC) does not recognize FFO as a primary measure of performance, and requires that companies reporting FFO also include a table in their financial statements that reconciles FFO to net income.

Generally Accepted Accounting Principles (GAAP): GAAP or Generally Accepted Accounting Principles are the widely accepted set of rules, conventions, standards, and procedures for reporting financial information, as established by the Financial Accounting Standards Board (in the U.S.).

Hedging: Used in the context here, hedging means protecting an investment position from adverse price movements. This is often used through the purchase and sale of "derivatives."

Initial Call Date: In most cases the Initial Call Date is five years from the Date of Issuance. The Call Date(s) and terms will be described in the prospectus, but the vast majority of REIT Preferreds may be first called by the issuer (in other words redeemed for the Call Price) five years from the date of issuance.

Initial Public Offering (IPO): A security's initial public offering (IPO) is the first offering of that security on the stock markets. The sale must be accomplished in conjunction with a prospectus that defines the provisions of the security and the background and financial condition of the issuer. The new shares are sold via one or more underwriters which then sell the shares to the public.

Interest: Distributions made periodically by companies to its lenders and note holders. These distributions are generally subject to contractual agreement, and missing a payment can have drastic consequences.

Investment Grade: Investment grade preferred or debt securities are considered to be securities that are rated in one of the four highest rating categories of a nationally recognized rating agency (e.g., between AAA and BBB by Standard & Poor's Corporation and Fitch IBCA, Inc. or between Aaa and Baa by Moody's Investors Service, Inc.),

Liquidation Value: The value assigned to each share of preferred stock in the event that the issuer is liquidated. Most often that value is $25.00. The ability of the investor to realize any value depends on the proceeds the company receives from its liquidation.

Mortgage REITs: Mortgage REITs act somewhat akin to banks and other lenders. They lend money to residential or commercial borrowers to finance real estate purchases. While this is a legitimate business model, these companies need to be evaluated separately to property-owning REITs, and are not a topic for this book.

Municipal Bonds: Bonds issued by state and local government entities. They differ from corporate bonds in that the interest paid to bond holders is generally free of federal income tax, and often free of state income tax to bond holders resident in the state of issuance.

Mutual Fund: A professionally managed pool of investments. Most often these are publicly traded securities that are actively traded by the mutual fund manager. The Fund is valued daily based on the price of the underlying securities, and investors can add to or liquidate their positions on a daily basis at the published closing price. Mutual funds invest in all types of public securities, depending on the focus described in the fund's prospectus.

National Association of Real Estate Investment Trusts (NAREIT) Equity Index: The "FTSE Nareit Equity REIT Index" is an index of the stock prices of all 112 U.S. Public Equity REITs (at the timing of writing: the index is updated quarterly). This excludes 27 mortgage REITs, which are not a subject of this book, and 15 REITs which are too small or illiquid to be included in most stock tables, and it is weighted by equity market capitalization. Note there are other REIT indices of stock prices published by various entities, including global indices, most notably the Morgan Stanley REIT Index, but the Nareit Equity Index quoted here is one of the most commonly used by investors.

Perpetual: Perpetual refers to securities that have no stated maturity date and will remain on the market until redeemed or called under whatever redemption provisions apply to the security.

Preferred Stock: Preferred stock is a hybrid equity security that has properties of both equity and debt. Preferreds are senior (i.e., higher ranking) to common stock, but are subordinate to debt. Preferred stock pays a dividend (not interest), and generally the preferred dividend has priority over the payment of a common stock dividend, and there are often penalties associated with an issuer missing payments of a preferred dividend. After several missed payments, these penalties can include the addition of directors representing the preferred shareholders, and limitations on the ability of the issuer making distributions to common shareholders. Most preferred stock carries no voting rights.

Most preferred stock issued by REITs is callable by the issuer after five years, and is otherwise perpetual (no maturity date).

Not included in this book is Convertible Preferred, which carries a feature permitting the preferred stock to be converted into common stock under some circumstances.

Similar to bonds, preferred stocks are often rated by the major credit rating companies.

Prospectus: As used in this book, the document filed with the SEC describing the key provisions, terms, and risks (as described by the issuer) of a security. A prospectus must comply with Securities Laws, and must be acceptable to the SEC. A Prospectus is the basic document that investors in a particular security should reference, and is available for all U.S. public companies on the SEC's EDGAR website.

Qualified Dividend: A qualified dividend is a dividend paid by a common or preferred stock that qualifies for the (at present) 15% tax rate of the U.S. income tax. REIT dividends are not qualified dividends.

Quantitative Easing: Actions by the Fed to increase liquidity, a form of printing money. Generally regarded as inflationary.

Quantum on Line: The website Quantumonline.com is a useful free data base of information, including links to preferred prospectuses. Summaries of almost all REIT Preferreds are included, along with information on almost all outstanding Preferred issues. Some useful sorts are available. They request, and it is nice to send, a contribution to help with their expenses.

Rating Agency: Companies that provide a credit rating for public debt and preferred securities and for the issuers themselves which investors can use to evaluate the quality of investments. Each (credit) rating agency has its own credit rating (credit ranking) system. Fees are paid by the issuers of the securities to the rating agency. Principal rating agencies are Moody's, Standard & Poor's, and Fitch. Issuers and securities are generally categorized by the rating agencies into those that are above or below investment grade, and sometimes securities carry 'split-ratings:' the securities may be rated as investment grade by one rating agency, but below investment grade by another.

Real Estate Investment Trust (REIT): A company that owns income-producing real estate and is structured in a manner (approved by the IRS) such that it does not pay federal corporate income taxes. Income from the REIT is in effect 'passed through' to the shareholders, in a similar manner to income from a partnership, which is 'passed through' to the partners. In this book we are only covering U.S. REITs whose shares are traded on the public stock exchanges such as the New York Stock Exchange.

There are limitations and requirements placed on the businesses and investments of REITs; among other requirements they are required to distribute 90% of their net income annually to shareholders, and the practice has been to distribute close to or more than 100% of available cash flow.

Redeem or Redemption: An issuer may redeem a preferred security in accordance with the provisions specified in the prospectus that was issued at the time of the initial public offering. To redeem a security, the issuer must pay the holder the redemption price that was specified in the IPO prospectus. Most recently issued Preferreds have redemption prices equal to the liquidation preference which normally is equal to the original issue price. Most recently issued securities cannot be redeemed for five years from the date of issue. The older Preferreds on the market can generally be redeemed any time since redemption restrictions have long since expired.

Securities and Exchange Commission (SEC), EDGAR: The primary mission of the U.S. Securities and Exchange Commission, generally referred to as the Securities and Exchange Commission or the SEC, is to protect investors and maintain the integrity of the securities markets. With the Securities Exchange Act of 1934, Congress created the Securities and Exchange Commission. The Act empowers the SEC with broad authority over all aspects of the securities industry. This includes the power to register, regulate, and oversee brokerage firms, transfer agents, and clearing agencies as well as the nation's securities self regulatory organizations. EDGAR stands for the Electronic Data Gathering, Analysis, and Retrieval system which performs automated collection, validation, indexing, acceptance, and forwarding of submissions by companies and others who are required by law to file forms with the SEC. All issuers of publicly traded securities are required to issue certain reports, and file them with the SEC using EDGAR. Accessing these reports on-line is simple using the SEC's website, www.sec.gov/edgar.shtml.

Step Up: In the context of this book, a provision in the preferred stock prospectus that in the event of 'Waldenization' (see below) the dividend rate will increase the Preferred stock of the acquired company.

Strip Yield: The current yield.

UPREIT (Umbrella Partnership REITs): Most, but not all, REITS are organized as Upreits. Most of the REITs assets are owned in a partnership (an "Upreit" unit) on a tax-deferred basis. The owners of Upreit units can exchange these Upreit units for common shares of the REIT, and have most of the same economic interest as shareholders. However, there can be conflicting interests, but these are generally not of sufficient importance to be of concern to most preferred shareholders.

Waldenization: One of the biggest, if not THE biggest, risk of investing in REIT Preferreds. A process by which the issuer of a Preferred goes private by selling its common shares to a private owner, but leaves the Preferred Shares outstanding. The private owner loads additional debt ahead of the Preferred investor, so the value of the Preferred shares is catastrophically reduced. The risk can be somewhat mitigated by investing in REIT Preferreds that have some 'change of control protection' and through diversification (spreading risk amongst a large number of stocks).

Yield: Yield is the amount of money returned to investors on their investments and is also known as Rate of Return. At the IPO of a security, the Yield would be equal to the Coupon Rate. After the IPO, the term Yield could be used to mean the Current Yield, the Yield to Call, the Yield to Maturity or the Yield to Worst (see below).

Yield to Call: Yield to call of a security is the yield if you were to buy and hold the security until the call date. This yield is valid only if the security is actually called at the call date. The calculation of yield to call is based on the distribution or coupon amount, the length of time to the call date, and the current market price. The yield to call value is only meaningful prior to the call date of the security. The value is also only meaningful if the market price of the security is above or possibly slightly below the call price of the security.

Yield to Worst: Yield to worst is the worst yield applicable to a security. For a preferred stock, which has no stated maturity, the yield to worst is the lesser of either yield to call or the current yield.

Appendix A

This is the portfolio of REIT Preferred shares that I owned as of 12-15-10. Note that some of these are still owned because I have a large taxable gain; otherwise, I would replace some with higher yielding REIT Preferreds. Don't necessarily use these as a guide, as I will be reviewing and likely changing my portfolio from time to time.

Simon Wadsworth's portfolio of REIT Preferreds at 12-15-10							
	Dividend	Price	Yield	TNX*	Spread over TNX	Corp Rating	Fixed Chge Coverage
AHT+D	$2.11	$23.19	9.1%	3.50%	5.61%		2.17
AIV-PU	$1.94	$25.44	7.6%	3.50%	4.12%	BB+	1.60
BDN-PD	$1.84	$24.80	7.4%	3.50%	3.93%	BBB-	2.23
BMR-PA	$1.84	$25.00	7.4%	3.50%	3.87%	BBB- Baa3	2.23
CBL-PC	$1.94	$24.54	7.9%	3.50%	4.40%		2.07
CBL-PD	$1.84	$23.51	7.8%	3.50%	4.34%		2.07
CDR-PA	$2.21	$25.11	8.8%	3.50%	5.30%		1.77
CUZ-PA	$1.94	$24.70	7.8%	3.50%	4.34%		1.46
CWH-PD	$1.63	$21.25	7.6%	3.50%	4.15%	BBB	1.97
DDR-PI	$1.88	$24.40	7.7%	3.50%	4.19%	BB	1.67
FR-PJ	$1.81	$20.40	8.9%	3.50%	5.38%	BBB-	1.69
GRT-PG	$1.66	$24.28	6.8%	3.50%	3.32%	BBB-	1.69
KRC-PF	$2.03	$24.39	8.3%	3.50%	4.83%	B+	1.31
LHO-PD	$1.95	$24.25	8.0%	3.50%	4.54%	BBB-	2.55
LXP-PB	$1.88	$25.03	7.5%	3.50%	3.99%		3.58
NRF-PB	$2.01	$19.63	10.3%	3.50%	6.75%		1.87
PKY-PD	$2.06	$24.95	8.3%	3.50%	4.77%		
SHO-PA	$2.00	$24.60	8.1%	3.50%	4.63%		2.04
SLG-PD	$2.00	$25.40	7.9%	3.50%	4.37%		1.50
Average			8.07%		4.57%		

*10-year bond yield mid-December 2010

Chart 29

CASH IS KING

Appendix B

Cogdell Spencer Series A Preferred Prospectus: December 17th, 2010

Highlights of provisions that provide some change of control protection to owners of Preferred Shares

C O G D E L L ✚ S P E N C E R

2,600,000 Shares

8.500% Series A Cumulative Redeemable Perpetual Preferred Stock
(Liquidation Preference $25.00 Per Share)

Upon the occurrence of a "fundamental change," you will have the right to convert some or all of your shares of Series A Preferred Stock into a number of shares of our common stock per $25 liquidation preference (inclusive of accrued and unpaid dividends) equal to the quotient of such liquidation preference plus an amount equal to accrued and unpaid dividends to, but not including, the fundamental change conversion date, divided by the market price of our common stock, par value $0.01 per share, which we refer to as our common stock.

Conversion Rights

Upon the occurrence of a fundamental change, you will have the right (the "fundamental change conversion right") to convert some or all of your shares of Series A Preferred Stock on the relevant fundamental change conversion date into a number of shares of our common stock equal to the quotient of the $25.00 per share Series A Preferred Stock liquidation preference plus an amount equal to accrued and unpaid dividends (whether or not earned or declared) to, but not including, the fundamental change conversion date, divided by the

---

CASH IS KING

market price of our common stock. All shares of our common stock delivered upon conversion of Series A Preferred Stock will be freely transferable without restriction under the Securities Act (other than by our affiliates).

We will not issue fractional shares of common stock upon the conversion of shares of our Series A Preferred Stock. Instead, we will pay the cash value of such fractional shares.

A "fundamental change" will be deemed to have occurred at such time after the original issuance of the Series A Preferred Stock when the following has occurred:

(1) the acquisition by any person, including any syndicate or group deemed to be a "person" under Section 13(d)(3) of the Exchange Act, of beneficial ownership, directly or indirectly, through a purchase, merger or other acquisition transaction or series of purchases, mergers or other acquisition transactions of shares of our stock entitling that person to exercise 50% or more of the total voting power of all shares of our stock entitled to vote generally in elections of directors (except that such person will be deemed to have beneficial ownership of all securities that such person has the right to acquire, whether such right is currently exercisable or is exercisable only upon the occurrence of a subsequent condition); and

(2) following the closing of any transaction referred to in clause (1) above, neither we nor the acquiring entity has a class of common securities listed on the NYSE, the NYSE Amex Equities, or NYSE Amex, or the NASDAQ Stock Market, or NASDAQ, or listed on an exchange that is a successor to the NYSE, NYSE Amex or NASDAQ.

The "market price of our common stock" will be the average of the closing price per share of our common stock on the 10 trading days up to but not including the effective date of a fundamental change.

Within 15 days following the occurrence of a fundamental change, we will provide to the holders of Series A Preferred Stock and our transfer agent a notice of the occurrence of the fundamental change, the resulting fundamental change conversion right and our right to exercise our fundamental change optional redemption right. Such notice will state:

- the events constituting the fundamental change;
- the date of the fundamental change;
- the last date on which the holders of Series A Preferred Stock may exercise their fundamental change conversion right;
- that we may elect to repurchase some or all of the shares of our Series A Preferred Stock as to which the fundamental change conversion right may be exercised;
- the method and period for calculating the market price of our common stock;
- the fundamental change conversion date;
- if applicable, subject to the succeeding paragraph, the type and amount of consideration entitled to be received per share of Series A Preferred Stock as if the conversion of the Series A Preferred Stock into common stock occurred concurrently with the occurrence of the fundamental change;
- the name and address of the paying agent and the conversion agent; and
- the procedures that the holders of Series A Preferred Stock must follow to exercise the fundamental change conversion right.

Notwithstanding the foregoing, in the case of a fundamental change as a result of which the holders of our common stock are entitled to receive stock, other securities, other property or assets (including cash or any combination thereof) with respect to or in exchange for our common stock, a holder of shares of our Series A Preferred Stock will be entitled thereafter to convert such shares of our Series A Preferred Stock into the kind and amount of stock, other securities or other property or assets (including cash or any combination thereof) which the holder of shares of our Series A Preferred Stock would have owned or been entitled to receive upon such fundamental change as if such holder of our Series A Preferred Stock held a number of shares of our common stock equal to the conversion rate in effect on the effective date for such fundamental change, multiplied by the number of shares of our Series A Preferred Stock held by such holder. In the event that the holders of our common stock have the opportunity to elect the form of consideration to be received in such fundamental change, we will make adequate provision whereby the holders of shares of our Series A Preferred Stock will have a reasonable opportunity to determine the form of consideration into which all of the shares of our Series A Preferred Stock, treated as a single class, will be convertible from and after the effective date of such fundamental change. Such determination will be based on the weighted average of elections made by the holders of shares of our Series A Preferred Stock who participate in such determination, will be subject to any limitations to which all of our holder of our common stock are subject, such as pro rata reductions applicable to any portion of the consideration payable in such fundamental change, and will be conducted in such a manner as to be completed by the fundamental change conversion date.

We will also issue a press release for publication on the Dow Jones & Company, Inc., Business Wire or Bloomberg Business News (or, if such organizations are not in existence at the time of issuance of such press release, such other news or press organization as is reasonably calculated to broadly disseminate the relevant information to the public), or post notice on our website, in any event prior to the opening of business on the first trading day following any date on which we provide such notice to the holders of our Series A Preferred Stock.

The "fundamental change conversion date" will be a date no less than 20 days nor more than 35 days after the date on which we give the notice described above. To exercise the fundamental change conversion right, the holder of Series A Preferred Stock must deliver, on or before the close of business on the fundamental change conversion date, the Series A Preferred Stock to be converted, duly endorsed for transfer, together with a written conversion notice completed, to our transfer agent. The conversion notice will state:

- the relevant fundamental change conversion date;
- the number of shares of Series A Preferred Stock to be converted; and
- that the Series A Preferred Stock is to be converted pursuant to the applicable provisions of the Series A Preferred Stock.

Notwithstanding the foregoing, if the Series A Preferred Stock is held in global form, the conversion notice must comply with applicable procedures of The Depository Trust Company, or DTC.

Holders of Series A Preferred Stock may withdraw any notice of exercise of their fundamental change conversion right (in whole or in part) by a written notice of withdrawal delivered to our transfer agent prior to the close of business on the business day prior to the fundamental change conversion date. The notice of withdrawal must state:

- the number of withdrawn shares of Series A Preferred Stock;
- if certificated shares of Series A Preferred Stock have been issued, the certificate numbers of the withdrawn shares of Series A Preferred Stock; and
- the number of shares of the Series A Preferred Stock, if any, which remain subject to the conversion notice.

Notwithstanding the foregoing, if the Series A Preferred Stock is held in global form, the notice of withdrawal must comply with applicable DTC procedures.

Series A Preferred Stock as to which the fundamental change conversion right has been properly exercised and for which the conversion notice has not been properly withdrawn will be converted into shares of common stock in accordance with the fundamental change conversion right on the fundamental change conversion date, unless we have elected to repurchase such Series A Preferred Stock by exercising our right to repurchase shares of our Series A Preferred Stock upon exercise of a holder's fundamental change conversion right. If we elect to redeem Series A Preferred Stock that would otherwise be converted into common stock on a fundamental change conversion date, such Series A Preferred Stock will not be converted into common stock and the holder of such shares will be entitled to receive from us $25.00 per share plus accrued and unpaid dividends (whether or not earned or declared) to, but not including, the date of redemption.

The holder of any shares of Series A Preferred Stock that we have elected to redeem and as to which the conversion election has not been previously properly withdrawn will receive payment of the fundamental change redemption price promptly following the later of the fundamental change conversion date or the time of book-entry transfer or delivery of the Series A Preferred Stock. If the paying agent holds cash sufficient to pay the fundamental change redemption price of the Series A Preferred Stock on the business day following the fundamental change conversion date, then:

- the Series A Preferred Stock will cease to be outstanding and dividends will cease to accrue (whether or not book-entry transfer of the Series A Preferred Stock is made or whether or not the Series A Preferred Stock certificate is delivered to the transfer agent); and
- all of the other rights of the holder of our Series A Preferred Stock will terminate (other than the right to receive the fundamental change redemption price upon delivery or transfer of the Series A Preferred Stock).

Subject to the immediately succeeding sentence, the aggregate number of shares of common stock issuable in connection with the exercise of the fundamental change conversion right may not exceed 15,632,500 shares of common stock (or 17,977,375 shares if the underwriters' over-allotment option is exercised in full) (the "Exchange Cap") resulting in a maximum number of shares of common stock per share of Series A Preferred Stock of 6.0125, which may result in a holder receiving value that is less than the liquidation preference of the Series A Preferred Stock. This is equivalent to a minimum market price of approximately \$4.158. The Exchange Cap is subject to pro rata adjustments for any stock splits or combinations with respect to our common stock.

In connection with the exercise of any fundamental change conversion right, we will comply with all U.S. federal and state securities laws and stock exchange rules in connection with any conversion of Series A Preferred Stock into common stock. Notwithstanding any other provision of our Series A Preferred Stock, no holder of shares of our Series A Preferred Stock will be entitled to convert such Series A Preferred Stock for shares of our common stock to the extent that receipt of such shares of common stock would cause such holder (or any other person) to exceed the common stock ownership or the aggregate stock ownership limit contained in our charter, subject to exceptions for persons subject to Excepted Holder Ownership Limits as defined in our charter.

These fundamental change conversion and redemption features may make it more difficult for or discourage a party from taking over our company. We are not aware, however, of any specific effort to accumulate our stock with the intent to obtain control of our company by means of a merger, tender offer, solicitation or otherwise. In addition, the fundamental change redemption feature is not part of a plan by us to adopt a series of anti-takeover provisions. Instead, the fundamental change conversion and redemption features are a result of negotiations between us and the underwriters.

We could, in the future, enter into certain transactions, that would not constitute a fundamental change but would increase the amount of debt outstanding or otherwise adversely affect the holders of our Series A Preferred Stock. The incurrence of significant amounts of additional debt could adversely affect our ability to service our debt, and to permit us to elect to repurchase the Series A Preferred Stock upon a fundamental change.

Optional Redemption

We may not redeem our Series A Preferred Stock prior to December 20, 2015, except in certain limited circumstances relating to the ownership limitation necessary to preserve our qualification as a REIT or in connection with our right to redeem our Series A Preferred Stock upon the exercise of a fundamental change conversion right by a holder as described above or in connection with our fundamental change optional redemption right as described below. For further information regarding these exceptions, see "— Conversion Rights" above, "— Fundamental Change Optional Redemption" below, and "Description of Common Stock — Restrictions on Ownership and Transfer" and "Description of Preferred Stock — Restrictions on Ownership" in the accompanying prospectus. On or after December 20, 2015, we, at our option upon not less than 30 nor more than 60 days written notice, may redeem our Series A Preferred Stock, in whole, at any time, or in part, from time to time, for cash at a redemption price of $25.00 per share, plus all accrued and unpaid dividends thereon (whether or not earned or declared) to, but not including, the date fixed for redemption.

A notice of optional redemption (which may be contingent on the occurrence of a future event) will be delivered not less than 30 nor more than 60 days prior to the redemption date, addressed to the holders of record of our Series A Preferred Stock at their addresses as they appear on our stock transfer records. A failure to give such notice or any defect in the notice or in its mailing will not affect the validity of the proceedings for the redemption of any shares of Series A Preferred Stock except as to the holder to whom notice was defective or not given. Each notice will state:

- the redemption date;
- the redemption price;
- the number of shares of Series A Preferred Stock to be redeemed;
- the place or places where the certificates, if any, representing the shares of Series A Preferred Stock are to be surrendered for payment; and
- that dividends on the shares to be redeemed will cease to accrue on such redemption date.

If fewer than all the shares of Series A Preferred Stock held by any holder are to be redeemed, the notice mailed to such holder will also specify the number of shares of Series A Preferred Stock to be redeemed from such holder. If fewer than all of the outstanding shares of Series A Preferred Stock are to be redeemed, the shares to be redeemed shall be selected by lot or pro rata or by any other equitable method we may choose.

Fundamental Change Optional Redemption

Upon the occurrence of a fundamental change, in addition to our right to redeem some or all of the shares of our Series A Preferred Stock upon the exercise by a holder of its fundamental change conversion right, we will have the option (the "fundamental change optional redemption right") to redeem our Series A Preferred Stock, in whole but not in part, within 90 days after such fundamental change for cash at $25.00 per share plus accrued and unpaid dividends (whether or not earned or declared) to, but not including, the date of redemption (the "fundamental change redemption price").

A notice of redemption will be delivered not less than 30 nor more than 60 days prior to the redemption date, addressed to the holders of record of our Series A Preferred Stock at their addresses as they appear on our stock transfer records. A failure to give such notice or any defect in the notice or in its mailing will not affect the validity of the proceedings for the fundamental change redemption of the shares of Series A Preferred Stock except as to the holder to whom notice was defective or not given. Each notice will state:

- the fundamental change redemption date;
- the fundamental change redemption price;
- the place or places where the certificates, if any, representing the shares of Series A Preferred Stock are to be surrendered for payment; and
- that dividends on the shares will cease to accrue on such fundamental change redemption date.

General Provisions Applicable to Redemptions

On the redemption date, we must pay on each share of Series A Preferred Stock to be redeemed any accrued and unpaid dividends, in arrears, for any dividend period ending on or prior to the redemption date. In the case of a redemption date falling after a dividend payment record date and prior to the related payment date, the holders of Series A Preferred Stock at the close of business on such record date will be entitled to receive the dividend payable on such shares on the corresponding dividend payment date, notwithstanding the redemption of such shares prior to such dividend payment date. Except as provided for in the two preceding sentences, no payment or allowance will be made for unpaid dividends, whether or not in arrears, on any Series A Preferred Stock called for redemption.

If full cumulative dividends on our Series A Preferred Stock and any Parity Shares have not been paid or declared and set apart for payment, we may not purchase, redeem or otherwise acquire Series A Preferred Stock in part or any Parity Shares other than in exchange for Junior Shares; provided, however, that the foregoing shall not prevent the purchase by us of shares held in excess of the limits in our charter in order to ensure that we continue to meet the requirements for qualification as a REIT. See "Description of Common Stock — Restrictions on Ownership and Transfer" and "Description of Preferred Stock — Restrictions on Ownership" in the accompanying prospectus.

On and after the date fixed for redemption, provided that we have made available at the office of the registrar and transfer agent a sufficient amount of cash to effect the redemption, dividends will cease to accrue on the shares of Series A Preferred Stock called for redemption (except that, in the case of a redemption date after a dividend payment record date and prior to the related payment date, holders of Series A Preferred Stock on the dividend payment record date will be entitled on such dividend payment date to receive the dividend payable on such shares on the corresponding dividend payment date), such shares shall no longer be deemed to be outstanding and all rights of the holders of such shares as holders of Series A Preferred Stock shall cease except the right to receive the cash payable upon such redemption, without interest from the date of such redemption.

Our secured revolving credit facility prohibits us from redeeming or otherwise repurchasing any shares of our capital stock, including the Series A Preferred Stock, during the term of the secured revolving credit facility.

Appendix C

Kite Realty Series A Preferred Prospectus:
December 17th, 2010

Highlights of provisions that provide some change of control protection to owners of Preferred Shares

2,600,000 Shares

8.250% Series A Cumulative Redeemable Perpetual Preferred Shares
(Liquidation Preference $25.00 Per Share)

We are offering 2,600,000 of our 8.250% Series A Cumulative Redeemable Perpetual Preferred Shares, par value $0.01 per share, which we refer to as our Series A Preferred Shares. This is our original issuance of our Series A Preferred Shares, and we have no other preferred shares outstanding as of the date hereof.

Dividends on our Series A Preferred Shares will be cumulative from the date of original issue and payable quarterly in arrears on or about the 1st day of each March, June, September and December, beginning on March 1, 2011, at the rate of 8.250% per annum of their liquidation preference, which is equivalent to $2.0625 per annum per share. If following a change of control of our company, either our Series A Preferred Shares (or any preferred shares of the surviving entity that are issued in exchange for our Series A Preferred Shares) or the common shares of the surviving entity, as applicable, are not listed on the New York Stock Exchange, or NYSE, or quoted on the NASDAQ Stock Market, or NASDAQ (or listed or quoted on a successor exchange or quotation system), holders of our Series A Preferred Shares will be entitled to receive cumulative cash dividends from, and including, the first date on which both the change of control occurred and either our Series A Preferred Shares (or any preferred shares of the surviving entity that are issued in exchange for our Series A Preferred Shares) or the common shares of the surviving entity, as applicable, are not so listed or quoted, at the increased rate of 12.250% per annum of the liquidation preference of our Series A Preferred Shares (equivalent to $3.0625 per annum per share) for as long as either our Series A Preferred Shares (or any preferred shares of the surviving entity that are issued in exchange for our Series A Preferred Shares) or the common shares of the surviving entity, as applicable, are not so listed or quoted. The first dividend on our Series A Preferred Shares sold in this offering is payable on March 1, 2011 (in the amount of $0.48697917 per share).

Dividends

Holders of Series A Preferred Shares will be entitled to receive, when, as and if authorized by our Board of Trustees, out of funds legally available for payment, and declared by us, cumulative cash dividends at the rate of 8.250% per annum per share of their liquidation preference (equivalent to $2.0625 per annum per Series A Preferred Share). However, if following a change of control of our company (as defined below), either our Series A Preferred Shares (or any preferred shares of the surviving entity that are issued in exchange for our Series A Preferred Shares) or the common shares of the surviving entity, as applicable, are not listed on the NYSE or quoted on NASDAQ (or listed or quoted on a successor exchange or quotation system), holders of our Series A Preferred Shares will be entitled to receive, when and as authorized by our Board of Trustees and declared by us, out of funds legally available for payment, cumulative cash dividends from, and including, the first date on which both the change of control has occurred and either our Series A Preferred Shares (or any preferred shares of the surviving entity that are issued in exchange for our Series A Preferred Shares) or the common shares of the surviving entity, as applicable, are not so listed or quoted at the increased rate of 12.250% per annum of the liquidation preference of our Series A Preferred Shares, equivalent to $3.0625 per annum per Series A Preferred Share for as long as either our Series A Preferred Shares (or any preferred shares of the surviving entity that are issued in exchange for our Series A Preferred Shares) or the common shares of the surviving entity, as applicable, are not so listed or quoted. The first dividend on our Series A Preferred Shares sold in this offering is payable on March 1, 2011 (in the amount of $0.48697917 per share).

Dividends on each Series A Preferred Share will be cumulative from the date of original issue and are payable quarterly in arrears on or about the 1st day of each March, June, September and December; provided, however, that if any dividend payment date falls on any day other than a business day, as defined in the Series A Preferred Shares Articles Supplementary, the dividend due on such dividend payment date shall be paid on the first business day immediately following such dividend payment date. Each dividend is payable to holders of record as they appear on our share records at the close of business on the record date, not exceeding 30 days preceding the corresponding payment dates thereof as fixed by our Board of Trustees. Dividends are cumulative from the date of original issue or the most recent dividend payment date to which dividends have been paid, whether or not in any dividend period or periods we shall have funds legally available for the payment of such dividends. Accumulations of dividends on our Series A Preferred Shares will not bear interest and holders of our Series A Preferred Shares will not be entitled to any dividends in excess of full cumulative dividends. Dividends payable on our Series A Preferred Shares for any period greater or less than a full dividend period will be computed on the basis of a 360-day year consisting of twelve 30-day months. Dividends payable on our Series A Preferred Shares for each full dividend period will be computed by dividing the annual dividend rate by four.

No dividend will be declared or paid on any Parity Shares unless full cumulative dividends have been declared and paid or are contemporaneously declared and funds sufficient for payment set aside on our Series A Preferred Shares for all prior dividend periods; provided, however, that if accrued dividends on our Series A Preferred Shares for all prior dividend periods have not been paid in full or a sum sufficient for such payment is not set apart, then any dividend declared on our Series A Preferred Shares for any dividend period and on any Parity Shares will be declared ratably in proportion to accrued and unpaid dividends on our Series A Preferred Shares and such Parity Shares. All of our dividends on our Series A Preferred Shares, including any capital gain dividends, will be credited first to the earliest accrued and unpaid dividend.

Our Board of Trustees will not authorize and we will not (i) declare, pay or set apart funds for the payment of any dividend or other distribution with respect to any Junior Shares (other than in Junior Shares) or (ii) redeem, purchase or otherwise acquire for consideration any Junior Shares through a sinking fund or otherwise (other than a redemption or purchase or other acquisition of our common shares made for purposes of an employee incentive or benefit plan of our company or any subsidiary, or a conversion into or exchange for Junior Shares or redemptions for the purpose of preserving our qualification as a REIT), unless all cumulative dividends with respect to our Series A Preferred Shares and any Parity Shares at the time such dividends are payable have been paid or funds have been set apart for payment of such dividends.

As used herein, (i) the term "dividend" does not include dividends payable solely in Junior Shares on Junior Shares, or in options, warrants or rights to holders of Junior Shares to subscribe for or purchase any Junior Shares, and (ii) the term "Junior Shares" means our common shares, and any other class of our shares of beneficial interest now or hereafter issued and outstanding that ranks junior as to the payment of dividends or amounts upon liquidation, dissolution and winding up to our Series A Preferred Shares.

A "change of control" shall be deemed to have occurred at such time as (i) the date a "person" or "group" (within the meaning of Sections 13(d) and 14(d) of the Exchange Act) becomes the ultimate "beneficial owner" (as defined in Rules 13d-3 and 13d-5 under the Exchange Act, except that a person or group shall be deemed to have beneficial ownership of all voting shares that such person or group has the right to acquire regardless of when such right is first exercisable), directly or indirectly, of voting shares representing more than 50% of the total voting power of our total voting shares; (ii) the date we sell, transfer or otherwise dispose of all or substantially all of our assets; or (iii) the date of the consummation of a merger or share exchange of our company with another entity where (A) our shareholders immediately prior to the merger or share exchange would not beneficially own, immediately after the merger or share exchange, shares representing 50% or more of all votes (without consideration of the rights of any class of shares to elect trustees by a separate group vote) to which all shareholders of the corporation issuing cash or securities in the merger or share exchange would be entitled in the election of trustees, or where (B) members of our Board of Trustees immediately prior to the merger or share exchange would not immediately after the merger or share exchange constitute a majority of the Board of Trustees of the corporation issuing cash or securities in the merger or share exchange. "Voting shares" shall mean shares of any class or kind having the power to vote generally in the election of trustees.

Symbol	Issue Date	Ex Div Date	Price	Shs Out	Current Yield	Yield to Worst Call	Yield to Call	Callable	Fixed Chg. Ratio	Moody's	S&P
MULTIFAMILY											
AIV U	3/24/2004	12/29/2010	25.61	12,000	7.6%	N/A	N/A	Y	1.44	Ba3	B+
AIV T	7/31/2003	12/29/2010	25.66	6,000	7.8%	-21.0%	-21.0%	Y	1.44	B3	B+
AIV V	9/29/2004	12/29/2010	25.63	3,450	7.8%	8.4%	N/A	Y	1.44	Ba3	N/A
AIV Y	12/21/2004	12/29/2010	25.71	3,450	7.7%	8.2%	N/A	Y	1.44	Ba3	B+
BRE C	3/15/2004	12/13/2010	24.34	4,000	6.9%	7.2%	N/A	Y	2.17	Baa3	BB+
BRE D	12/9/2004	12/13/2010	24.18	3,000	7.0%	7.3%	N/A	Y	2.17	Baa3	BB+
EQR N	6/19/2003	12/16/2010	24.05	6,000	6.7%	7.0%	N/A	Y	2.31	Baa2	BBB-
PPS A	10/1/1996	12/13/2010	53.50	868	7.9%	8.7%	8.8%	Y	3.25	N/A	BB
PPS B	10/28/1997	12/13/2010	25.00	1,986	7.6%	7.7%	23.7%	Y	3.25	N/A	BB
UDR G	5/31/2007	1/12/2011	24.62	3,406	6.9%	6.5%	6.5%	Y	2.06	Baa3	BB+
SELF STORAGE											
PSA A	3/31/2004	12/13/2010	24.19	4,600	6.3%	6.2%	28.7%	Y	5.26	Baa1	BBB+
PSA C	9/13/2004	12/13/2010	24.23	4,425	6.8%	7.1%	N/A	Y	5.26	Baa1	BBB+
PSA D	2/28/2005	12/13/2010	23.61	5,400	6.5%	6.7%	N/A	Y	5.26	Baa1	BBB+
PSA E	4/27/2005	12/13/2010	24.30	5,650	6.9%	7.2%	N/A	Y	5.26	Baa1	BBB+
PSA F	8/23/2005	12/13/2010	24.17	9,893	6.7%	6.9%	N/A	Y	5.26	Baa1	BBB+
PSA G	12/12/2005	12/13/2010	25.05	4,000	7.0%	N/A	N/A	Y	5.26	Baa1	BBB+
PSA H	1/19/2006	12/13/2010	24.90	4,200	7.0%	7.0%	N/A	Y	526	Baa1	BBB+
PSA I	5/3/2006	12/13/2010	25.06	20,700	7.2%	7.5%	17.2%	Y	5.26	Baa1	BBB+
PSA K	8/812006	12/13/2010	25.06	16,990	7.2%	2.3%	2.3%	Y	5.26	Baa1	BBB+
PSA L	10/20/2006	12/13/2010	24.75	8,267	6.8%	7.1%	12.7%	Y	5.26	Baa1	BBB+
PSA M	1/9/2007	12/13/2010	24.39	19,065	6.8%	2.1%	2.1%	Y	5.26	Baa1	BBB+
PSA N	7/2/2007	12/13/2010	25.11	6,900	7.0%	4.6%	4.6%	Y	5.26	Baa1	BBB+
PSA O	4/13/2010	12/13/2010	25.85	5,800	6.6%	6.0%	6.0%	Y	5.26	Baa1	BBB+
PSA P	10/7/2010	3/11/2011	24.55	5,000	6.6%	7.0%	8.2%	Y	5.26	Baa1	BBB+
PSA W	10/6/2003	12/13/2010	24.19	5,300	6.7%	7.1%	N/A	Y	5.26	Baa1	BBB+
PSA X	11/13/2003	12/13/2010	23.98	4,800	6.7%	7.1%	N/A	Y	5.26	Baa1	BBB+
PSA Z	3/5/2004	12/13/2010	23.91	4,500	6.5%	6.9%	N/A	Y	5.26	Baa1	BBB+
FOCUSED OFFICE											
ARE C	6/29/2004	12/29/2010	25.73	5,186	8.1%	2.5%	2.5%	Y	3.44	N/A	N/A
AREEP	3/26/2008	12/29/2010	24.50	10,000	7.1%	7.3%	N/A	N	3.44	N/A	N/A
BMR A	1/18/2007	12/29/2010	25.05	9,000	7.4%	7.5%	8.3%	Y	2.27	Ba1	N/A
BDN C	12/30/2003	12/28/2010	24.85	2,000	7.5%	8.1%	N/A	Y	2.10	N/A	N/A
BDN D	2/27/2004	12/28/2010	24.86	2,300	7.4%	8.0%	N/A	Y	2.10	Ba1	N/A
OFC G	8/11/2003	12/29/2010	25.33	2,100	7.9%	8.2%	N/A	y	2.07	N/A	N/A
OFC H	12/18/2003	12/29/2010	25.20	2,000	7.4%	7.8%	N/A	Y	2.07	N/A	N/A
OFC J	7/20/2006	12/29/2010	25.20	3,390	7.6%	7.2%	7.2%	Y	2.07	N/A	N/A
CHW C	2/9/2006	10/28/2010	23.79	6,000	7.5%	8.1%	N/A	Y	1.99	Baa3	BB+
CHW D	10/11/2006	10/28/2010	21.22	15,180	7.7%	7.1%	N/A	N	1.99	Baa3	BB+

Index